It's Your
ENVIRONMENT

Things to Think About — Things to Do

from THE ENVIRONMENTAL ACTION COALITION

ILLUSTRATED BY SUSAN HULSMAN BINGHAM

Edited by Sherry Koehler

 Charles Scribner's Sons   New York

Acknowledgments

The Environmental Action Coalition wishes to thank the many people, associations, organizations, government agencies, educational institutions, and corporations that have provided so much help over the years in publishing Eco-News, the magazine from which the chapters of this book have been taken. Some provided help with content . . . Laurence Pringle, Judy Rothstein, Ceil Lipschitz, Al Bradford, Michelle Burke, Betty Kahn, the Girl Scout Council of Greater New York, New York Botanical Garden, Bicycle Institute of America, and the Council on the Environment of New York. Others provided illustrations . . . Bernice Mast; Beth Greer; our wonderful regular illustrator, Susan Hulsman Bingham; and also Richard Stahl, whose sweet potatoes and carrots enhance the "City Farming" chapter of this book.

Others--members of the staff of EAC since 1970--provided just about everything . . . ideas, writing talent, inspiration, long hours, hard work, faith, and love. To them, especially Joan Edwards, Kristin Bergfeld, Nancy Wolf, Roger Guttentag, Karen Greenberg, Karen Dumont, Sherry Koehler, Marcia Hornstein, Sarah Batty, Terry Randall, and Ronnie Cohen, we extend warmest thanks and appreciation.

Copyright © 1976, 1975, 1974, 1973, 1972, 1971 The Environmental Action Coalition, Inc.

Environmental Action Coalition.
  It's your environment.
SUMMARY: Text, illustrations, and suggested projects explore environmental concerns of urban areas.

1. Environmental protection—Juvenile literature. 2. Pollution—Juvenile literature. 3. Recycling (Waste, etc.)—Juvenile literature. 4. Nature conservation—Juvenile literature. [1. Environmental protection. 2. Pollution. 3. Recycling (Waste) 4. Conservation of natural resources] I. Bingham, Susan Hulsman. II. Koehler, Sherry, III. Title.
TD 170.2.E58 1976 301.31 75-39302; ISBN 0-684-14626-6; ISBN 0-684-14625-8 pbk.

1 3 5 7 9 11 13 15 17 19 M D/C 20 18 16 14 12 10 8 6 4 2
1 3 5 7 9 11 13 15 17 19 M D/P 20 18 16 14 12 10 8 6 4 2
Printed in the United States of America

Contents

Introduction

Talking and reading about the environment can often be a gloomy business. Much of our environment is in a lot of trouble-- especially the environment of cities. We read about it and hear about it every day.

But the environment--even in cities--is not all gloomy. People can learn to enjoy their environment, no matter where they are. They can observe it more closely. They can understand how people's behavior affects it. They can make practical every- day decisions to protect and improve it. The can PARTICIPATE.

That's why the Environmental Action Coalition began in 1971 to publish an environmental newsletter for young people, called Eco-News. Eco-News was conceived especially for children living in or near cities. It encourages them to become partici- pants in their environment, not only by exploring it, but also by seeking solutions to its problems.

Eco-News has claimed a wide audience of young readers who take great pleasure in its clever and funny illustrations, and its straight-forward, informal style. Their response has prompted us to bring the best issues of Eco-News together into this book,

It's Your Environment. We have provided, we think, enough to keep children happily occupied for months.

Teachers and students will be natural users of the book, as many of the topics and activities fit readily into the curriculum at levels from the lower grades through junior high. Scout troops, camps, youth organizations, and community groups will also find a wealth of useful ideas for discussions, programs and projects. The book is designed so that the reader may plunge into it at any chapter that's of interest. Solid waste, transportation, energy, dog litter, birds, butterflies--each chapter, like each issue of Eco-News, is a separate and easily-digestible unit.

In It's Your Environment we suggest activities that are practical and timely. Caring for street trees, cleaning up a vacant lot, growing plants, recycling bottles and cans, and conserving energy at home and school, are positive and immediate steps toward a better and cleaner environment.

But It's Your Environment also stresses the future...the need to plan, to understand cause and effect, to involve families and communities, to translate immediate environmental improvement into long term environmental gain.

It's Your Environment is, in a sense, a young beginner's manual for environmental action. We hope it is only the start of a growing urge among the young people who read it, to understand more fully, and participate more actively in the wonderful environment that sustains us all.

THE ENVIRONMENTAL ACTION COALITION

CHAPTER ONE

Grandma Was an Ecologist

Times are changing. People are changing. And the environment is changing, too. Many of the changes in our world are good changes. Many diseases can now be cured. People don't have to work as hard at certain kinds of jobs. But the world around us is changing in some frightening ways, too. For one thing, the world is getting more polluted.

Change isn't always good. Things aren't always better because they are new. Often we can learn a great deal from old ways.

Think about things you can do to stop pollution. Use less electricity. Buy recycled products. (These are products made from material that has already been used.) Recycle your paper, bottles, and cans by taking them to a "recycling center." Reuse things. Make things yourself instead of buying them. Now think about what you have read in history books about how people lived years ago. Environmentalists who study and work to protect the environment are really saying, "Sometimes the old ways are best for our environment."

That is why we say grandma was an ecologist. She didn't think of herself as an ecologist. (People didn't use that word in those days.) We don't mean that she never polluted. (Sometimes she polluted more than we do. Look at all the air pollution she caused by burning coal.) But we can learn some things about how to protect our environment from the way grandma lived.

Let's take a little peek at grandma's time. Let's see some of the things she did that helped the environment. (Even though she didn't know it.)

PACKAGING

We all know that packag-
ing can cause garbage
problems. Stores were different when your grandmother
shopped. Packages were
different too.

On this page are pictures of
things people bought years ago.
What do the pictures tell you about
packaging in grandma's time? Which
things were sold loose instead of in
many separate little packages? Which
things were not packaged? Which
things were left in "nature's
packaging?" Do you see any "bubble
packs," those cardboard cards with
plastic bubbles on them?

Investigate some more on your own. Look
for pictures of stores in history books.
Interview older people. Ask them what
packaging was like years ago. How was it
different from today? Here are some
questions you might ask.

1. How were cheese and meat packaged?

2. Did soda come in disposable bottles?

3. Were containers made of plastic?

4. What kind of a container did milk come in?

5. Were there many frozen foods? If there weren't,
why not? (Do frozen foods use a lot of packaging?)

6. How were hardware stores different than they are
today? Were items packaged differently?

Think about the differences between packaging today and
years ago. Did grandma use a lot of packages? Do you use more?
Did she make more garbage? Or is there more garbage today?

POWER POLLUTES

Electricity

Every time you use electricity you are causing a little pollution. The power plants that make electricity for your home pollute the air or water.

Grandma used electricity. But she didn't use as much as we do now. She didn't have as many appliances and gadgets. Electric toothbrushes. Electric can openers. Electric pencil sharpeners. Electric combs. All these things are new inventions. All of them cause pollution when we use them. But grandma didn't use them at all.

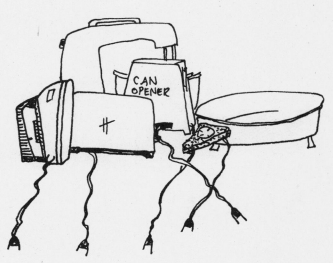

Make a list of all the things in your home that use electricity. How often do you use them? Are there some that you could use less often? Try!

Automobiles

Cars, cars, cars, and more cars! Today, cars are all around us, polluting the air we breathe. And what about roads? We keep building more roads to drive on. Ugly cement highways are gobbling up more land every day.

Years ago, most people in cities used trolley cars and buses instead of cars. They rode bicycles. They took trains. They walked a lot.

Today, people who care about the environment are asking us to use cars less. They say that we should travel on buses, subways, and trains. This is called <u>mass transportation</u>. When many people travel together in one vehicle, there is less pollution from power. And we don't need as many parking lots or big highways. Another solution to automobile pollution is to use more muscle power. How often do you walk or ride a bike? It's healthier. And muscle power doesn't pollute at all!

3

MAKE IT LAST

What do you do when something is worn out, torn or broken? You probably throw it away. But why? Many old things can become as good as new when they are repaired.

In grandma's time people didn't throw things away as fast as we do today. They made things last. When clothing ripped, they sewed it up. When furniture broke, they repaired it. Making repairs took time and effort, but many useful things were kept out of the garbage that way.

MAKE IT YOURSELF

What do we do when we want something new to wear, some tasty jam for breakfast, a new toy? We usually buy it!

Grandma bought a lot of things too. But she also made many things herself. She made jams, jellies, and other preserves. She sewed clothes for the whole family. She made a lot of her own hand creams, perfumes, and other cosmetics. She didn't often buy pesticides or insecticides. Instead, she used her own "home remedies" to get rid of house and garden pests. They worked--and they didn't harm the environment!

When you make things yourself, you usually use fewer wasteful packages. You often reuse old things instead of throwing them away. You can take special care to use good healthy ingredients in your home-made food. You'll probably save money. And best of all, making things yourself can be fun!

4

RECYCLE IT

Grandma recycled. She used things more than once. Sometimes she used them for new purposes. "Junk" was valuable in her time. There were many junk and scrap dealers around.

Years ago it was easier to recycle some things. For instance, in grandma's time, scrap dealers sold cotton rags made from old clothing to paper mills. The cotton rags could be used to make paper. But nowadays most of our clothing is made from <u>synthetic</u> materials. These are materials such as nylon and orlon that are made from chemicals rather than plants. Synthetic materials cannot be used to make paper. So they are not recycled.

Today you can recycle some of the things you use. You can take your bottles, cans, and newspapers to a recycling center near you. If there isn't one, start a recycling center in your school or community. Read Chapter Eight to learn how.

NEW USES FOR OLD THINGS

Grandma made many of her own toys when she was young. She probably made a wagon from an old wooden crate, some roller skate wheels, and leftover lumber. She made rag dolls and stuffed animals from old cloth. She covered her textbooks with old paper bags or wrapping paper instead of buying new book covers.

 When grandma grew up she kept right on reusing things. She made pretty quilts from old pieces of fabric. She brought her own shopping basket to the store instead of using up lots of paper bags. She made picture books for her children by cutting up old magazines. (And she pasted them with homemade flour-and-water paste.)

When grandma reused things, she made their life longer. She kept things out of the garbage.

5

DISPOSE OF DISPOSABLES

<u>Disposables</u>. These are things that are made to be thrown away. Popcorn-making kits. No-deposit, no-return bottles. Disposable diapers. Grandma didn't use them. She used cloth napkins that could be washed and reused. She used china plates, instead of paper ones. She used returnable, refillable bottles.

When was the last time you went to a big birthday party? Think of all the disposables that were used at the party. Paper plates. Paper napkins. Plastic spoons and forks. Candy baskets. How many things were thrown away after the party instead of being saved and reused for the next birthday? It was easier to clean up, of course. Disposables are convenient. You can use them and throw them away without thinking about them. But remember, they don't really disappear. They end up being burned in our incinerators or buried in our garbage dumps and landfills.

TWO THINGS TO THINK ABOUT

1. Grandma worked hard. Would you work a little harder to help the environment? Would you clean up after your party if there weren't any disposables? Would you take your recyclables to a recycling center? Would you repair your broken toys instead of buying new ones?

2. Don't exaggerate. Remember, not all modern changes are bad. Many are very helpful. They make our lives safer and healthier and more comfortable. Make a list of the good changes that help us, but that don't pollute.

CHAPTER TWO

How Does Energy Affect Your Life?

You probably know that we are in an "energy crisis."
People are trying to save energy. They are afraid there
will not be enough fuel to heat our homes in the winter.
They might have to use their cars less. They feel that
their lives are going to change.

There are a lot of reasons
for the energy crisis:

1. <u>We want and use more
energy.</u> Your family uses
more energy than your grandmother's family did. Think
of the things around your
house that use electricity.
Could you get along without
some of these things?

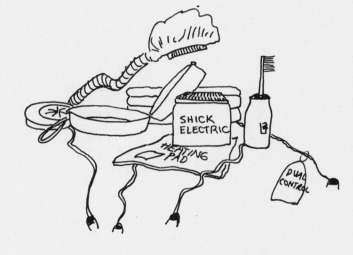

2. <u>There are more people
today than when your grandmother was young.</u> More
people use more energy.
The people in the United
States use twice as much
energy today as they did
ten years ago.

3. <u>We waste energy</u>. We want big cars that need more fuel than smaller cars. We leave lights on all over the house even when we don't need them. We forget to turn radios and TV's off when we are finished watching and listening.

4. <u>Some of our fuels are now in very short supply</u>. We gobble up fuel without thinking about where it comes from. It is becoming difficult to get enough fuel for all our machines.

The way we use energy <u>can</u> change our lives. Some of these changes are good. Others are not so good. This chapter will help explain what energy is. It will explain some of the ways energy affects <u>your</u> life. The next time you hear people talking about the energy crisis, you will understand more about how it all came about.

WHAT IS ENERGY?

Energy Is All Around . . .

People have been using the word
"energy" a lot recently. But do you
know what it really means? Have you
seen any energy as you've walked
around your neighborhood? Have you
smelled, touched, or tasted energy?
How do we know that such a thing as
energy is really there?

Not even the smartest scientists
know exactly what energy _is_. But we
know a lot about what energy _does_. We
see the results of energy all around us,
every day. ENERGY GIVES A FORCE THAT
DOES WORK. This force pushes or pulls
something from one place to another.

Sometimes energy changes as it does work.
But this doesn't mean that it is gone. It is
still there in another form. For example, the
stored energy in wood changes to the energy of
heat as the wood burns.

. . . And You Have Some of It

Did you know that _you_ have energy?
You do. And you can see how you use your
energy in many ways. Pick up a pencil
from your desk. You have just used some
of your energy. Your energy gave you the
force to pull the pencil and move it from
one place to another.

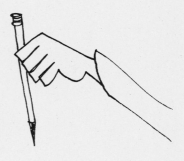

All day you use your energy to move and
to change things. That way, you can do
the things you want to do. You can't
see this energy, but you can see the
results of its action. Can you think of
other ways you use your energy every day?

Your Energy Waits to Be Used

Energy can be stored until you
are ready to use it. Where does your
energy come from? Energy is stored
in your muscles. As your stored energy
is used up, you become tired. You must
then rest and build up more energy to use.

9

Your "Fuel" Helps You to Store More Energy

After your body uses up its stored energy, how does it get more? A machine receives fuel such as coal or oil to do its work. Your body's "fuel" is the food you eat. Your food comes from other animals and from plants. These animals and plants have stored energy. As you digest your food, its stored energy is absorbed by your body. Then it is stored in your muscles, ready to be used at a later time.

Plantlife Is Where the Action Really Is

For you, and for other animals, the important source of fuel is plantlife. Plants get their energy from the sun. They use sunlight in a process called <u>photosynthesis</u>. The green <u>chlorophyll</u> in plants traps the sun's energy and uses it to make <u>glucose</u>. Glucose is a kind of plant sugar. It is the main fuel that plants use to do their work.

Plants store some of the energy they get from the sun. When you eat your lettuce and tomato salad, you are actually eating some of the sun's energy to help make your own.

All our energy comes from the sun. It is called <u>solar energy</u>. Without solar energy, nothing could be done. Nothing could exist.

ENERGY NEVER GOES AWAY

NEW PLANTS

What about all the stored energy in plants and animals that never get eaten by other creatures? What about your <u>own</u> stored energy that may never get used up? Does all this stored energy just go away?

Energy never goes away. It is always being moved and changed into different forms.

SOLAR ENERGY'S WORK

Imagine the earth without the sun's heat and light. It would be dark, cold, and lifeless. The sun's energy makes the earth livable.

All energy does work. Solar energy does many important jobs on earth. It does them so well that we hardly pay attention to them. Yet the sun's work is going on every day.

Solar Energy and the Air

Nearly all of the sun's energy goes off into space. A small fraction does not. It comes to the earth. The earth's air gets solar energy first. The air acts like a mirror and a sponge. Some solar energy is reflected away from the earth. Some is absorbed.

This absorbed solar energy becomes heat. It warms the air. The air begins to rise and move around. This warm air can force cold air to move too. We feel this moving air as the winds.

Winds Are Important

Ocean water is also warmed by solar energy. But the water will not move around as much as warm air. The wind's force can push ocean water for long distances. (Have you noticed that beach waves are much higher on windy days?)

The water that is pushed by the wind becomes the ocean currents. These currents move the warm and cool water around. Coastlines are kept warm or cold by these currents.

Not Too Hot, Not Too Cold

Not all places receive the same amount of solar heat. The North and South Poles get very little. Other places, such as the tropics, get much more solar heat. Ocean currents and winds help to even out the earth's weather. Otherwise, it would be too extreme. The tropics would be much hotter. And the poles would be much colder.

NATURAL CYCLES

Every day the earth recycles. Land is destroyed. New land is made. Living things die. New life is born. How is this possible? It happens through nature's system of <u>natural cycles</u>. Natural cycles make new things from old over and over again. Everything would soon be used up without them. Solar energy keeps our natural cycles going.

Water Cycle

The water cycle is the simplest natural cycle. Solar energy evaporates ocean water. The water becomes water vapor. On a hot day we can feel this water vapor.

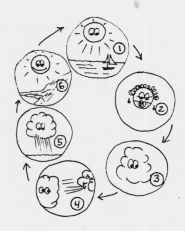

Water vapor gathers into clouds. Many clouds are pushed over the land by the winds. When they become cool, they turn into rain.

On the land, some of the rain runs into rivers and streams. Rivers and streams eventually flow into the sea. Then the cycle begins again.

Mineral Cycles

There are many minerals living things need. Iron and salt are two examples. But minerals are often buried within the earth. How do they get into living things?

Winds and moving water rub like sandpaper. Year after year they rub rocks and soil. This rubbing action is called <u>erosion</u>.

During erosion, many minerals are brought to the surface of the earth. They become part of the soil. Plants are then able to use them.

Minerals are also washed or blown into the earth's waters. When they are dissolved in water, they can be used by both plants and animals.

After plants and animals die, their bodies decay. As they decay, the minerals in their bodies are released to the earth again. And the cycle begins anew.

12

Carbon and Oxygen Cycles

Plants and animals are part of two important cycles. They are the carbon and oxygen cycles.

All food contains carbon. Carbon helps hold the captured solar energy. When living things need energy, they "burn" food. This uses oxygen.

Oxygen is a gas which all animals breathe in. Oxygen joins up with the carbon. Together they make carbon dioxide (CO_2). This is the gas animals breathe out.

Carbon dioxide is then used by plants during photosynthesis. From it, plants make their food. Photosynthesis releases oxygen to the air. Both cycles are completed.

LEARN MORE BY YOURSELF

"Sealed World," an Example of Balance in a Natural Community

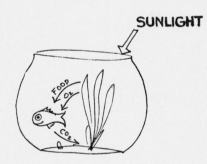

You can have fun learning more about the carbon and oxygen cycles. Make a sealed world and see how plants and animals give each other carbon dioxide and oxygen. (We learned about this project from the High Rock Nature Conservation Center in Staten Island, New York.)

Nature will not allow too many plants and animals to exist in one space or "community." Each plant and animal must have enough food, water, and space to take care of its needs. This is called the "balance of nature." You can see for yourself how a community of plants and animals can stay in balance.

Equipment You Will Need

A one-gallon, wide-mouth glass jar with lid
Small amount of sandy soil or 1 1/2" aquarium gravel
Pond water
4 or 5 water plants (such as eel grass and elodea, easily obtained in any aquarium shop)
1 snail
2 minnows, each not more than 1" long
Paraffin

What to Do

Put sandy soil or gravel in bottom
  of jar.
Plant water plants in soil or gravel.
Fill jar with pond water to within
  2" of top.
Allow one week for soil, water, and
  plants to settle.
Add snail and minnows.
Seal with paraffin. Be sure to screw
  lid on jar before pouring in paraffin.
Keep jar in good light, but not in
  direct sunlight.

Observing Your Experiment

You do not have to do anything for your "sealed world."
It should be able to maintain itself in natural balance
without any help. But do protect it from hot sunlight or freezing
cold.

What Is Really Happening

The green plants carry on photosynthesis by using light
from the sun. They also use minerals from soil, water, and
the carbon dioxide given off by the fish and the snail. The
plants give off oxygen which the fish and snail need in order to
breathe.

The plankton (tiny plants that live in the water) keep
multiplying. This makes a steady food supply for the fish
and snail. The snail is a scavenger. It feeds on the tiny
plants growing on the glass. It feeds on the larger plants,
too.
The animals give off carbon dioxide. This is used by
the plants.

Each plant and animal gives something to the "sealed
world." All together, they create a balanced community.

HOW HAVE PEOPLE USED ENERGY?

Early People Discovered Natural Energy

In their earliest days, people were wanderers. They gathered berries, hunted animals, and caught fish to live. They used their own muscles to do all their work. They got energy from the food they ate. But you can imagine how tired they got! There had to be an easier way!

Perhaps one day a man caught a clam from the edge of the ocean. He tried to open it, but it was difficult to do with just the strength of his hands. How could he increase his force? He decided to try a rock. To his delight, the added strength and weight of the rock gave the energy of his muscles more force. He had discovered that he could add to his body's force.

People soon discovered that the energy in wood could be changed to heat. Heat kept them warm and cooked their food. It also melted metals so they could be shaped into tools and weapons. Heat from wood was a new energy source to add to peoples' energy and increase their force.

People also realized that animals could help them do work. They used the muscular energy of animals to carry loads and to operate simple tools for harvesting crops and grinding grain. People were still using their own muscular energy. But they were also using the muscles of stronger animals. The energy still came from food. But now it came from the food the animals ate as well as the food that people ate.

This didn't solve all of the problems, though. People still had to feed and take care of their animals. Animals weren't strong enough to do <u>all</u> the work that needed to be done. They couldn't do it <u>fast</u> enough. They were expensive. They grew old and died.

Machines Increased Energy

Simple machines were invented. Some of these machines got their energy from the wind or falling water. Windmills and waterwheels helped grind grains. But the wind didn't always blow. When it didn't blow, people couldn't use its energy. And since they didn't always live near fast-moving streams, they couldn't always use water's energy to move the waterwheels.

Over two hundred years ago, new kinds of energy began to be used to power machines. This was the beginning of what is called the Industrial Revolution. New machines burned fuels to do work. The energy of muscles, wind, and water was replaced with the chemical energy in fuels. People moved to towns and cities to be near the machines. Some people say that the Industrial Revolution was really an "energy revolution." This is because new ways were found to get and use energy. This began to change the world.

At first, wood was used for fuel to power the new machines. But people quickly changed to coal, oil, and natural gas. These are called fossil fuels. They were formed from plants and animals buried millions of years ago. The stored energy of these plants and animals is still in the fuel. Burning releases the stored energy as heat. And where did the energy of the plants and animals come from? It came from the true source of all energy in the world--the sun.

Soon people began to have many machines to do work in their homes. This was possible because a way to generate electricity had been invented. Most of the energy to produce electricity comes from fossil fuels. The fuel boils water, the water creates steam, the steam turns the turbines and electricity is generated.

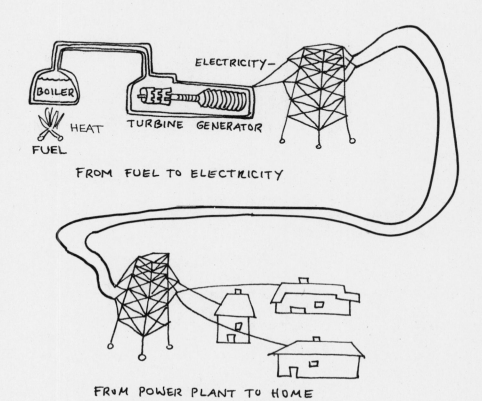

FROM FUEL TO ELECTRICITY

FROM POWER PLANT TO HOME

People wanted more and more machines. Homes, factories, and transportation changed and grew.

What does all this mean? It means that energy can change the way people live. Nowadays we depend on machines to do many things for us. We use up more and more energy every year. We have an energy crisis because we are running out of fuel to power all our machines. And we live in a more polluted world because burning fossil fuels dirties our environment.

WHY SHOULD WE CONSERVE ENERGY?

In the United States, we depend almost completely on fossil fuels for heating, for electricity, and for transportation. We are being asked to use less fuel because the United States doesn't have enough supplies of oil and natural gas. But there are other reasons to conserve energy. Fossil fuels can cause many problems. Using them can harm the environment.

FOSSIL FUELS HARM THE ENVIRONMENT

Fossil Fuels Cause Land Pollution

When coal is mined, the land around the mines is often torn up. The topsoil is pushed away and erosion causes landslides. Sometimes even houses are covered. Many trees are cut down and this increases erosion. The land looks very bare and ugly. Oil and gas pollute the land when there are spills around the drilling area. When there are breaks in pipelines, oil is spilled. Plants cannot grow where the oil spills.

Fossil Fuels Cause Water Pollution

Oil and gas spills from offshore drilling and tanker collisions may pour many gallons of oil into the water. This kills fish and other sea life. Acid from coal deposits can run into nearby streams, making them polluted.

Fossil Fuels Cause Air Pollution

Much coal has lots of sulphur in it. The sulphur releases poisonous gases into the air when the coal is burned. High-sulphur oil also has this problem. Burning coal puts many <u>particulates</u> into the air. Particulates are small pieces of soot. These particulates combine with poisons in the air to make it more polluted. Automobiles burn gasoline (made from fossil fuels) and put carbon monoxide into the air. Gasoline that contains lead puts lead particles into the air. Lead and carbon monoxide poison living things. Low-sulphur oil, natural gas, and non-leaded gasoline are cleaner fuels.

Fossil Fuels Put Extra Carbon Dioxide into the Air

All living things contain carbon. Remember that fossil fuels come from ancient living things. So fossil fuels have carbon also. Whenever we burn coal, natural gas, or oil, the carbon they have "joins up" with the oxygen in the air. Carbon dioxide (CO_2) is made. Animals do not use CO_2 at all. But plants need CO_2 for photosynthesis.

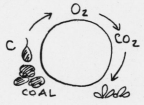

Since we are burning more fossil fuels today, much more CO_2 is going into the air. Some scientists think too much of anything is not good. They are worried that too much CO_2 in the air will change the earth's climate. Other scientists don't think this will happen, but they are not sure.

Fossil Fuels Heat Up the Atmosphere

We like heat when it keeps us warm. But many times heat can be a problem. Too much heat makes us uncomfortable. Too much heat in the water or air can make the environment change.

Whenever we use energy to do work, we also produce heat. (Don't you feel warmer when you run around a lot?) But we don't use all of this heat to do work. In this way, heat is sort of "leftover" energy.

"Waste" heat can pollute. In water, it can kill fish and other living things. Some scientists wonder if the extra heat in the air will someday make our climate hotter.

The extra heat produced by cars, factories, and air conditioners moves all over the world. (Do you remember what makes it move?) What would happen if it got warmer all over the world? Would some living things die? Would icecaps melt and cause floods?

No one knows for sure how this extra heat will affect our environment. But many scientists are worried. They want to learn more about "leftover" energy. They want to find out the answers before anything happens to harm our environment.

In the future we will have to think more carefully about the way we use energy. We will have to think more carefully about the way we live.

CHAPTER THREE

How Should We Use Energy?

People have been gobbling up energy for many years. More people are using more energy than ever. We are wasting energy. We are using fuels that pollute the earth.

But it doesn't have to be that way. We can change the way we live. We can learn not to waste energy. We can <u>conserve</u> our present forms of energy. We can also find new sources of energy that don't pollute. This chapter will show you some ways that you can help.

BUILDINGS AND ENERGY

It takes a lot of energy to heat homes, factories, and office buildings. People can conserve fuel for heating in many ways. For example, they can turn down thermostats and wear sweaters to keep warm.

But conserving fuel is easier in some buildings than in others. Some buildings use up more energy because of the way they are built. It is often easier and cheaper to build buildings that waste heating fuel. After all, architects and builders don't have to pay your heating bills!

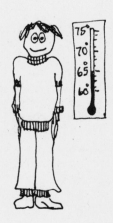

Let's look at some ways buildings can be designed to conserve fuel. Let's also look at ways people can conserve fuel after the buildings are built. The main thing is to <u>keep the cold air out and the hot air in.</u>

Use Lots of Layers

Think about how you dress in the winter-time. You wear many layers of clothing. These layers keep the cold air and wind away from your body. They also trap your body heat so that it can keep you warm.

Buildings with many layers do the same thing. For example, <u>insulation</u> adds layers to a building. Insulation is often made of fiberglass. It is put between the walls to keep cold out and heat in. Thick walls and roofs also protect buildings from cold winds and weather.

Buildings that are connected to each other also have more protection. The other buildings keep the cold out on two sides. It's like having super-thick walls! Storm windows, shutters, and curtains are extra layers for windows. Rugs on floors and tiles on ceilings are extra layers for floors and ceilings.

Work with Nature

Sometimes we don't want layers. We open curtains during the day to let the sun shine in. The sun helps heat the room. Then at night, we close the curtains again to keep the cold out and the heat in.

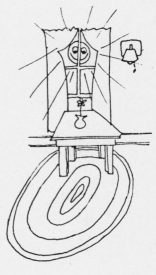

Stuff Up Cracks

Buildings can let in the cold in other ways. The wind can blow in under doors and around window frames that don't fit properly. Your parents can do something to keep wind and drafts out of rooms. They can put sticky stuff, called "putty," in the cracks. They can also put strips of metal on the bottoms of doors. This is called "weather-stripping."

Trap the Cold Air

Many homes and apartment buildings have two front doors. The space in between the doors is often called a <u>vestibule</u>. It traps the cold air before it has a chance to get in the building.

LEARN MORE BY YOURSELF

Are You a Heating-Fuel Waster?

Ask yourself these questions:

Windows

1. How many windows are there in your house or apartment?

2. How many have shutters?

3. How many have curtains that open and close?

4. How many have storm windows or thermopane? (Thermopane is a special kind of glass with two layers.)

5. How many have putty in the cracks?

6. How many have plastic sheets over them?

Doors

1. How many doors are there in your house or apartment?

2. Does your house or apartment building have a vestibule?

3. How many doors let air in under them?

4. How many have weatherstripping at the bottom?

Floors and Ceilings

1. How many rooms are there in your house or apartment?

2. How many rooms have wood floors with no covering?

3. How many rooms have rugs?

4. How many rooms have tiles or linoleum on the floor?

5. How many rooms have tiles on the ceiling?

TRANSPORTATION AND ENERGY

The Problem

Many years ago, people used animal power, wind power, and their own muscle power for transportation. These forms of energy didn't harm the environment.

Today we use cars, planes, and other modern machines for transportation. These machines use fossil fuels for power. They also pollute the environment.

The Solution

Some kinds of transportation use up more fuel than others. People who drive cars use more fuel than people who ride trains or buses. So one solution is to use <u>mass transportation</u>. This is when many people ride together.

Another solution would be to use more muscle power. Bike or walk more. What's your hurry anyway?

We must find new ways to move people and things. We need transportation that doesn't cause noisy traffic jams. We need transportation that doesn't pollute. We need transportation that doesn't waste energy.

Here are some transportation problems for you to solve:

1. We can't always travel by train or bus. Sometimes cars are necessary. But big, heavy cars need more fuel than smaller, lighter cars. Use this chart to compare cars. If a car weighs 2,000 pounds, how many miles per gallon does it get? If it weighs 4,000 pounds? If it weighs 5,000 pounds? Does your family own a car? How many miles per gallon does it get?

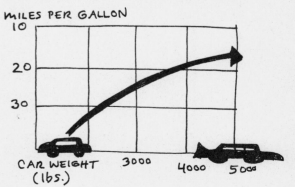

BIG CARS TAKE MORE GAS

MILES PER GALLON

CAR WEIGHT (lbs.)

2. This chart compares three kinds of transportation--planes, cars, and trains. The plane and train are each carrying 360 people. With 4 people in each car, 90 cars will also carry 360 people. Everyone is traveling 500 miles. The last column shows how much fuel the plane, train, and cars need.

Kind of Transportation	Miles Traveled	Number of Passengers	Gallons of Fuel
1 plane	500 miles	360 people	3,911 gallons
90 cars	500 miles	360 people	3,316 gallons
1 train	500 miles	360 people	1,238 gallons

Figure out how much fuel each <u>person</u> uses when he travels by plane, train, or car. It is easy to do. Just follow our example. Divide the number of people into the number of gallons each kind of transportation uses. Compare your answers. Which kind of transportation conserves the most fuel? Which wastes the most fuel? If each car only carried 2 people, which would waste the most fuel?

EXAMPLE: Traveling by train

$$\frac{1,238}{\text{gallons}} \cdot \frac{360}{\text{people}} = \frac{3.4}{\text{gal. per person}}$$

ELECTRICITY AND YOUR HOME

Something very exciting happened in 1882. Fifty-nine customers in New York City got electric lights from Thomas Alva Edison's Company.

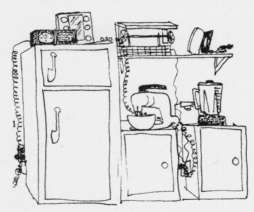

Things have changed a lot since then. Today our homes are filled with electrical gadgets and appliances. It is hard to imagine what our lives would be like without them.

Each year we use more and more electricity. But we forget that a power plant has to produce the electricity we use. Most of these power plants can't get enough fuel right now. And fossil fuels can cause pollution.

People should conserve energy in their homes. They should use less electricity. How can they do this? Have a discussion with your family. Make a list of your ideas for saving energy.

Many power companies can send you information and good conservation ideas. Write to Con Edison, 4 Irving Place, New York, N.Y. 10003, or to the power company in your city or town. Ask for pamphlets and posters about energy conservation.

NEW WAYS TO GET ENERGY

Everything man does uses energy. We can use less. But we will always have to use some energy. Fossil fuels are now our main source of energy. They are very easy to use. But burning fossil fuels pollutes our environment.

Fossil fuels are also limited. They can be used up. This is because no <u>new</u> fossil fuels are being made while we're using up existing supplies.

Solar Energy and the Future

All over the world, many people are experimenting with solar energy. They have very good reasons for doing this. If solar energy warms and lights the earth, why can't it warm and light our homes? Can it do other jobs like cooking, making fresh water, or generating electricity? Almost every day, enough solar energy falls on your home to do this work.

Using Natural Materials

Solar energy comes to us for free. The hard part is capturing it. Green plants have already solved this problem. One way to use solar energy is to have plants capture it for us. Then we can use what the plants produce.

One example is rubber. We used to take all the rubber we use from rubber trees. But now rubber is usually made from fossil fuels.

Rubber trees grow by solar energy. We can keep planting them. They will produce more rubber every year. They can't be used up as fossil fuels can. And we can save limited fossil fuel supplies for making things we cannot get from nature.

Collecting Solar Energy

Many people are learning how to capture solar energy so we can use it.

One way is to use materials that capture and hold the solar energy long enough for it to do its work. This work can be heating air or water. The materials are called <u>solar collectors</u>.

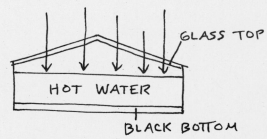

GLASS TOP

HOT WATER

BLACK BOTTOM

SOLAR WATER COLLECTOR

Make Your Own Solar Energy Collector

You can make your own small solar energy collectors. This experiment will help you see how a real collector would work.

Materials Needed

    2 tin cans of equal size
    black paint
    2 thermometers (optional)

Clean the cans you will be using. Be sure their tops are off. Paint the outside of one can black. Leave the other can unpainted.

Fill the cans with the same amount of <u>cold</u> water. If you have thermometers, place one in each can. Place the cans in direct sunlight for two to three hours. Then feel the water or look at the thermometers. Which can is warmer?

← PAINTED CAN

Try using other colors. Do blue cans collect solar energy better than black ones? How warm does the water get in the unpainted can? Try wrapping cans in aluminum foil or cotton. How does this affect the temperature of the water?

Which collector was the best? Why?

Concentrating Solar Energy

Another way man can capture solar energy is to use special mirrors. These special mirrors are shaped like shallow bowls. They concentrate solar energy like a magnifying glass. They can be used in places where the solar energy is not very strong.

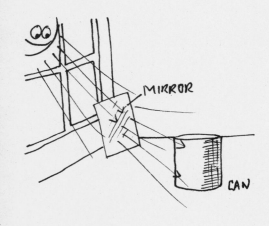

MIRROR

CAN

You can learn how mirrors reflect solar energy. Place a can filled with cold water in the shade. Place a mirror so that it will reflect sunlight on the can. Does the reflected sunlight warm the water? Is one mirror enough? Does this method capture solar energy better than tin-can collectors?

Geothermal Energy

Have you ever seen a picture of "Old Faithful" geyser in Yellowstone National Park? It is a natural hot-water fountain.

Deep inside, the earth is made of very hot <u>liquid</u> rock. Sometimes some of it comes near the earth's surface. It boils underground water. Sometimes this boiling water turns to steam. When the hot water or steam comes up through a crack in the earth, we call it a "geyser."

Sometimes the steam of the geyser is carried directly by pipes into buildings. In other cases it is used to generate electricity. If the steam is used to generate electricity, it is called <u>geothermal energy.</u> Many people like geothermal energy because it doesn't pollute. But right now it is usually too expensive and hard to use. We still have to find out more about it.

Gas from Coal

There is a lot of coal in the United States. But mining and using coal causes pollution. We might be able to get rid of these problems, though. One way is to change the coal to gas while it is still in the mine.

Many experiments are being done. One way to change coal to gas is to set the coal on fire underground. Then we can capture the gas that escapes while the coal burns. This is still too hard and expensive to do in the United States. In Europe, however, coal gas is used a lot. Maybe the United States will use it soon.

Atomic Energy

Fission Energy--Breaking Atoms Apart

Atoms are very small particles. You cannot see them but they are everywhere. Everything is made up of atoms. All atoms have energy. It is called "atomic energy."

We use atomic energy for certain purposes today. It is called <u>fission energy.</u> We break apart very large special atoms to get it. They are called <u>uranium atoms</u> and they are loaded with energy. When we break them apart, we get heat. We can use this heat to generate electricity.

FISSION ENERGY

ENERGY

URANIUM
ATOM

Try a little experiment with three people. It will help you understand fission energy. Two people pretend they are part of a uranium atom. One person holds their hands together. The uranium people cannot run away from each other. Why? Because the third person is holding them together. He represents energy. The energy in a uranium atom keeps it from breaking apart. Now let everybody drop hands. What is left? The energy, of course! Now the energy isn't needed to hold the uranium atoms together. It can turn to heat to make electricity.

Fusion Energy--Forcing Atoms Together

We could use atomic energy another way. It is called <u>fusion</u> energy. We force small atoms together to make it. The smallest atoms in the world are called <u>hydrogen.</u> When we force two hydrogens together we get a <u>helium atom.</u> We also get heat.

Let's use five people for another experiment. Two will be hydrogen atoms. A third will stand between them. He represents atomic energy. The two remaining will represent a strong outside energy. Can the two hydrogens come together by themselves? No, because there's atomic energy keeping them apart. Now let the outside energy people help force the two hydrogens together. The atomic energy in between is squeezed out. The two hydrogens can then form helium. The atomic energy is no longer needed to keep hydrogen atoms apart. It turns to heat. This heat can be used to generate electricity.

FUSION ENERGY

HYDROGEN   HYDROGEN

OUTSIDE   ATOMIC   OUTSIDE
ENERGY   ENERGY   ENERGY

Scientists understand how fusion energy works. But we can't produce it yet. Scientists think we will be able to in the future.

We are already producing <u>fission energy</u> in nuclear power plants. But some people don't like fission energy. They think the power plants are unsafe. They are also afraid of atomic wastes. These wastes are very poisonous. And they stay poisonous for thousands of years. Many people ask, "Where can we safely store these wastes? And for how long?"

Energy from Garbage

Some companies are burning garbage to help generate electricity. In this way, two problems may be solved. There will be more fuel for electricity. There will also be less garbage for cities to get rid of. (Be sure to read the next chapter, "Where Does All the Garbage Go?" to learn more about energy from garbage).

Companies are experimenting with ways to get energy from garbage. They know they have to burn the garbage without polluting.

We also know that the best way to save energy is not to be wasteful in the first place.

It takes a lot of energy to make the products you buy. Here are three ways to conserve energy when you buy products.

1. Buy things that last a long time. Don't waste the energy used to make them.

2. Buy soda in returnable containers. Returnable containers use up less energy than disposable ones.

3. Buy recycled paper. It takes less energy to make recycled paper than to make paper from trees.

CHAPTER FOUR

Where Does All the Garbage Go?

Garbage cans overflowing with paper, plastic, soda cans, orange peels, and coffee grounds . . . trucks in the early morning, groaning and clanking as the garbage is crushed inside . . . garbage men calling to each other as they toss rattling cans back onto the sidewalks. These are sights and sounds that are very familiar to city kids.

But what happens to the garbage after it is thrown into the trucks? People today throw away lots and lots of garbage. But few seem to know or care what happens to it.

Garbage is a problem. People who try to solve this problem call garbage by a special name--<u>solid waste</u>. Solid waste won't go away by itself. It can't disappear into water or air. Picking it up and taking it away is one of the most important jobs city workers do.

Getting rid of solid waste is called <u>disposal</u>. Sometimes disposal means that solid waste is just piled up in <u>open dumps</u> and left to sit there. Sometimes it is buried under several feet of dirt in <u>sanitary land-fills</u>. And sometimes it is burned in <u>incinerators</u>.

Let's take a look at some of the problems we have getting rid of our solid waste. Next time you see a garbage truck on your block, you will know where all the garbage goes!

THE OLD, OLD STORY OF GARBAGE

Was solid waste always a problem? How did people in "olden days" get rid of things they no longer wanted?

In the first place, there weren't as many people in long-ago times. They didn't have so much to throw away. They grew their own fruits and vegetables. They killed animals for meat. They didn't shop in stores, so they didn't need lots of packages.

Our ancestors made their own containers out of clay and plants. They used them over and over. They made simple, sturdy furniture to last for a long time. Worn-out clothes were made into rugs and quilts. Left-over food was eaten by the animals. People long ago had no need of huge garbage cans.

But some things _were_ thrown away. For example, when clay bowls broke, they became solid waste. They were thrown away in open dumps. At first, dumps were small. But as people settled down and built towns and cities, dumps became larger and larger. The first garbage men began to go from house to house with carts and horses. Solid waste began to be a real problem.

Today each of us throws away about four pounds of garbage every day. That adds up to 400,000 _tons_ a day in the whole country! Almost all of it is still dumped in the same way it was in "olden days." Only our dumps are much, much bigger. There are many more people today. And each of us throws away more and more each year.

WHAT ABOUT TODAY'S DUMPS?

As open dumps get bigger, they are using up valuable land that could be used for something better. For instance, some people might want to build houses or schools there.

People used to think that swamps, ditches, and big holes were perfect places to dump garbage. But now we know that many birds and water creatures start their lives in swamps. If we fill all of these natural places with garbage, many living things could become extinct. This means that there would not be any more of them, ever.

Another problem with open dumps is that they can catch fire. As food rots, it gives off heat. The heat may cause fires to start deep in the pile of garbage. Many dumps burn all the time. The result is lots of air pollution.

Open dumps also cause water pollution. As rain water trickles through the solid waste in a dump, it can pick up a lot of germs and chemicals. The polluted rain water then becomes part of the water table deep below the surface. Many of us get our drinking water from the water table, through wells and springs. If the water table is poisoned by dumps, people can become sick.

Dirty water may also drain into rivers and bays near open dumps. The polluted water often kills fish and other water creatures. It is not good for people to use.

ARE THERE ANY GOOD DUMPS?

Since open dumps cause so many problems, some large cities have started a new kind of dump. This is called a <u>sanitary landfill</u>. Solid waste is still hauled to a special place and dumped. But the garbage is not allowed to just sit there and cause pollution.

There are lots of huge machines at a sanitary land-fill. One of them is a <u>bulldozer</u>. The bulldozer spreads the solid waste out so it doesn't pile up in one spot.

A <u>sprayer truck</u> sprays all the waste with <u>disinfectant</u>. This chemical helps to keep the garbage from smelling bad. It keeps away the flies, mice, and rats that live so well in plain old dumps.

After the solid waste has been spread out and sprayed, the <u>earth-movers</u> push a layer of soil all over it. It is packed down. The layers of garbage and earth are built up like a sandwich.

After many years, when the landfill is high enough, it is covered over with a final thick layer of earth. Some of the things in it rot away. Food and other natural things turn into soil. But glass jars and aluminum cans don't rot. They remain as they are for many years.

After a long time, a sanitary landfill can be used for a park or golf course. But since the new land is soft, it cannot be used as a foundation for tall buildings.

No matter how carefully they are built, landfills still may cause the water table to become polluted. This happens from rainwater running through the garbage to the water below. And landfills still use up lots of valuable land near cities. So even though they are better than open dumps, they are still not the final answer.

GARBAGE TO BURN

Some cities burn solid waste. They have built giant buildings with enormous furnaces. These are called <u>incinerators</u>. Incinerators burn hundreds of tons of garbage a day. Many burn all day and all night.

When a garbage truck arrives at an incinerator, it backs up to the edge of a pit. The truck opens up and a huge blade pushes the waste out. It falls into the pit, which holds many tons of garbage.

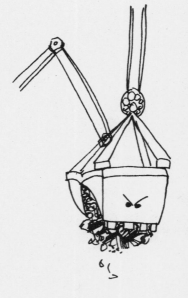

Overhead is a giant crane with a bucket shaped like a clam shell. This bucket comes down and scoops up some of the solid waste. Then the waste is dumped into a long chute that leads to the fire. Some things are hard to burn, so the fire is kept very, very hot. Paper, of course, burns easily. But wet food burns slowly. Some things, such as metals, may never burn completely.

The material that is left over after burning is called <u>residue.</u> About 20 percent of the solid waste that goes into the furnace is left over as residue. It makes a good clean material for landfill that packs down more firmly than unburned solid waste.

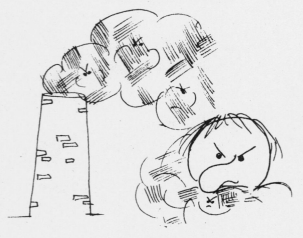

In the past, many incinerators have made smelly smoke. But nowadays most cities are adding equipment that takes out the dirt and keeps the air clean.

WHAT'S IN THE FUTURE?

What about our future?
Improper disposal of solid
waste causes air and water
pollution. It uses up good
land. Some interested people
are thinking about these
problems and they have come up
with some good solutions.

One thing we can do is stop throwing so many things away.
Instead, we can recycle newspapers, glass, tin cans, and aluminum
Recycling means that new paper, bottles, and cans will be made
from old ones.

Some cities and towns recycle newspapers. In New York
City special racks have been attached to many of the garbage
trucks. People separate newspapers from their other solid
waste. The tied bundles are put in the racks. They never get
dumped in the landfill. The paper is sold to make new newspaper
or cardboard.

Solid waste has also become a
valuable fuel. One garbage can of
solid waste has the fuel energy of
one gallon of gasoline. Since coal
and oil are now scarce and expensive,
solid waste is a good substitute,
either burned by itself or along with
coal or oil. The smoke from the
stacks can be cleaned so that there
will be no air pollution.

A big new plant that turns garbage into energy is being
built in Massachusetts. It is called a refuse-energy system.
It will burn solid waste in a huge furnace. The heat from the
fire will boil water in boilers to create steam. Then the
steam will be sent through a pipe to run machinery in a nearby
power plant. This will make electricity.

The left-over residue will be recycled. Iron will be
picked up by a magnet and sold to a steel mill. Glass can be
mixed with concrete to make construction materials. Even the
dust collected in the chimney can be sold to add to cement.
After the solid waste is used for energy and recycling, there
will be almost nothing left to dispose of.

LEARN MORE YOURSELF--MAKE YOUR OWN DUMP

Create your own dump and your own sanitary landfill. See for yourself what happens to garbage.

Equipment You Will Need

Two medium-sized plastic boxes
Enough soil to fill both boxes
    half full
Examples of solid waste, such as
    an apple, aluminum foil, card-
    board, glass, newspaper, tin-
    can lid

What to Do

    Put the soil in the boxes.
One box will be an open dump and
one a sanitary landfill. In the
dump, put one example of each
kind of solid waste. Just let it
sit there. Water it lightly from
time to time.

For the sanitary landfill, put one example of each kind of
solid waste into the box. Be sure to put them close to the
outside of the box so you can observe them. Cover the waste
with several inches of soil.

Observing Your Experiment

    Observe what happens
to both boxes. What
types of solid waste rot?
Does the same thing happen
to both boxes? What
differences do you notice?
OBSERVE THE EXPERIMENT
FOR SIX MONTHS.

CHAPTER FIVE

The Birth and Life of a Piece of Paper

How many kinds of paper can you think of?
Newspaper. Writing paper. Candy wrappers.
Subway posters. Paper bags.

Have you ever wondered how paper is made?
Most paper is made from trees. Lumbermen cut
the trees down. They saw the trees into logs
and bring them to a paper mill. At the mill
the bark is taken off the logs. Then the wood
is chopped into tiny pieces called chips.
These chips are mashed with water to make mushy
soup called <u>pulp</u>. Usually the pulp is mixed
with many chemicals and cooked before it is put
into a paper-making machine.

But what happens to used paper? Most paper goes into the
garbage after we have used it. It fills up our landfills and
dumps. Or it is burned in incinerators. No one uses it again.
Many people feel it is wrong to waste paper this way. They
think used paper should be made into pulp again and then into
new paper. The new paper would be <u>recycled paper</u>. Recycling
would make the life of paper longer.

Some paper these days is being recycled. New paper is
being made from old paper, not trees. Old paper is collected
and brought to a paper mill. Here it is chopped up and mixed
with water to make pulp. This is just like the pulp made out
of wood chips. Sometimes the ink is washed out of the old
paper. Then the pulp is put into the paper-making machine.

Recycled paper is good paper. It
is hard to tell that it is made from
used paper instead of trees. Some
newspapers are made from recycled
paper. Some stationery and paper
napkins, too. This book is made of
recycled paper. You can even buy
recycled birthday cards!

WHY SHOULD WE RECYCLE PAPER?

There Are More People Now and People Use More Paper

People use more paper today than they did years ago. We throw more things away. We buy fancier and bigger packages made out of paper. We use paper napkins, paper towels, paper plates and cups. Our grandparents didn't use them. There are also more people today. That means more and more trees have to be cut down to make paper to fill our needs.

Recycling Saves Trees

It takes 17 trees to make a ton of paper from wood. Recycled paper is made from other paper, not wood. If people buy paper made from paper instead of wood, they will be saving trees.

We Are Running Out of Trees

Paper companies plant new trees to replace the ones they cut down. They study how to make trees live longer and grow bigger. But it takes a long time for a tree to grow big enough to be used for paper. Some trees die before they can be used. And in the meantime people keep asking for more and more paper.

So paper companies need more trees. Today they are even cutting down trees in our national forests. Ten years from now we will probably need more trees than we can grow. What will we do then? SAVE A TREE. USE LESS PAPER. USE RECYCLED PAPER.

Recycling Helps Save Our Environment

If we recycle our paper we won't have to burn it in incinerators or dump it in landfills. Remember, people are worried about where to put all our garbage. Saving paper and recycling it keeps it out of the garbage.

WHAT IS RECYCLED PAPER MADE OF?

Many kinds of paper can be used to make new paper. Some companies use old newspaper to make new newspaper. Some use office paper. One paper company in Wisconsin has even discovered a way to make recycled paper from old milk cartons and ice cream packages. Next time you look at your milk carton in school, think of the recycled paper that can be made from it. The wax coating is taken off in a special process. The paper that is left is mashed up and rolled out into new paper for offices and schools.

The first time this company bought milk cartons from schools a funny thing happened. All the kids put their used milk cartons in special waste baskets at school. Then the cartons were put in a special machine to crush them. When the men turned the machine on, they got a funny feeling at their feet. Their feet were getting wet. Pretty soon they were standing in milk up to their ankles. No one had told the kids to empty out the cartons before they threw them away. PEOPLE HAVE TO BE TOLD HOW TO RECYCLE!

Different Papers Don't Get Along Together

There are many different kinds of paper. Each paper recycling company has to choose what kind of scrap paper it needs to make recycled paper. They need one kind of scrap paper to make school paper, another kind to make tissues, and still another kind to make newspapers.

Some paper mills are very fussy. For example, they might not want paper with a shiny coating on it. It means more work for them to wash the coating off. Some mills can mix up a few different kinds of paper. But first they must know what is there. It is like cooking. Each paper mill makes new paper with a special recipe.

39

WHAT DOES RECYCLED PAPER LOOK LIKE?

Recycled paper looks and feels the same as paper made from trees. There is recycled paper with the ink taken out. There is recycled paper with the ink left in.

When the ink is taken out of the old paper, the recycled paper is usually white. But when the ink is not taken out, the paper is gray or tan with little specks in it. Cardboard is made of old paper with the ink left in. Tear a piece of cardboard at the corner. You will see all sorts of specks of ink and coloring from old paper. You will also see many short pieces of paper mashed together.

PAPER PROJECTS

Save your paper and recycle it

Find out if there is a recycling center near you. Ask what kind of paper they collect. Then save paper and bring it to the center. Offer to help by working at the center.

Buy recycled paper

If no one buys recycled paper, all the old paper we collect will be wasted. The paper mills won't need it. Ask for recycled paper in stores. Give recycled paper as gifts.

Tell your parents and friends about recycled paper

Tell them to buy recycled paper instead of paper made from trees.

Do things with your class

Have a class project. Make posters telling the rest of the school about recycled paper. Write a play or puppet show about saving trees. Show it to the younger kids. Ask your teacher to find out if there are any recycled paper mills near your town that you can visit. Make paper together.

GIVE a
RECYCLED
BIRTHDAY
CARD
TODAY!

LEARN MORE BY YOURSELF--MAKE YOUR OWN PAPER

You can make new paper from old paper. Making your own paper is very much like what happens in a paper recycling mill. At a mill the pulp is put into a machine with a long moving screen. The water drips through the screen. Then the screen moves through parts of the machine that press and dry the pulp. Finally, there is new paper! To make your own recycled paper all you need are a few simple supplies.

Equipment You Will Need

    8-10 pieces of tissue or 2-3 pieces of used paper
A piece of screen about 3 inches square
A flat pan a little larger than the screen
3 or 4 pieces of white blotting paper the size of the
    screen
A bowl
An egg beater
A round jar
Newspaper
Instant starch (This is not necessary, but it will make
    the paper a little stronger.)

What to Do

1. Tear the tissue into very small bits in the bowl. Add 2 cups of hot water, and beat the tissue and water with the egg beater to make pulp.

2. If you want to use the starch, add 2 teaspoons of it to the pulp.

3. Pour the pulp into the flat pan.

4. Slide the screen into the bottom of the pan and move it around until it is evenly covered with pulp.

41

5. Lift the screen out carefully. Hold it level and let it drain for a minute. Then put the screen, pulp side up, on a blotter on some newspaper.

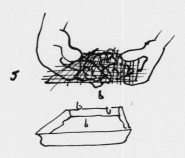

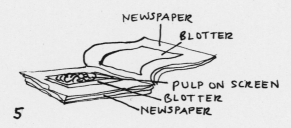

6. Put another blotter over the pulp, more newspaper over that, and roll the jar over it to squeeze out the rest of the water.

7. Take off the top newspaper. Turn the blotter sandwich over so that the screen is on top. Then take off the blotter and screen very carefully. Don't move the pulp! There is your paper. Put a dry blotter on the pulp and let the pulp dry. You have just made paper from paper!

CHAPTER SIX

Packaging, Packaging, and More Packaging

A sardine can. A milk carton. A shampoo bottle. The box your cousin's electric trains came in. The plastic and cardboard around your mother's thread. A piece of cellophane. An empty paper bag. A plastic bleach bottle. What do all these have in common? They are all PACKAGES.

Packages are part of the garbage that we throw away. We all know that garbage causes many pollution problems. It pollutes our air, water, and land.

Yet every day more and more things are put in packages. Every day the package designs get bigger and more complicated. And that means that we are creating more garbage to pollute our environment.

Do we really need all these packages? Sometimes the things we buy have too much packaging. Sometimes the packages are bigger than they have to be. Sometimes they are made of materials that make a lot of pollution when they are disposed of. Most packages can't be reused. Most are never recycled.

What can you do? First learn about packages. Some packages are better than others. They are easier to recycle. They make less garbage. They can be reused. They pollute less when they are burned in incinerators. Then learn how to be an "ecological" shopper. Consider packaging every time you go to the store.

WHY DO WE HAVE PACKAGES?

Most of the things we buy come in some kind of package. Packages keep things from spoiling. They keep things from spilling all over. They protect things. They make things fit neatly on a shelf. They make things easy to carry and hold. They make things look pretty.

There are many reasons for packages. That's why some people are paid a lot of money to design packages for products.

PACKAGING YESTERDAY

People didn't always have the packages we have today. Think about all the different kinds of packages you have seen in history books and movies. Ancient civilizations stored their food and water in clay pots and woven baskets. Years ago, general stores had big barrels, bags, and boxes filled with food.

When the first settlers came to the United States, they lived on or near farms. They grew most of their own food or they bought it from their neighbors. They made most of their own clothes and furniture. Packages weren't too important.

As cities grew, it was harder to get fresh food. The farms were farther away from the cities. People invented ways to keep food from spoiling while it traveled to the cities. Packages helped protect food.

City workers wanted to buy more things. They didn't have time to make things themselves. More and more products were invented. Each product needed a different kind of package.

44

PACKAGING TODAY

The world is changing, people are changing, and packaging is changing, too.

People today are in a hurry. They are too busy to return bottles to a store. They want foods that are quick and easy to cook. They want to use paper napkins, towels, and dishes that don't have to be washed. Use it and throw it away. That's how we think.

The things we use and throw away are called "disposables." Disposables don't just disappear when the garbage man takes them. They get burned or buried in landfills. They cause pollution.

Every year new products are invented, and most of them come in packages. Manufacturers design attractive packages so you will want to buy their products. Packages today are bigger and fancier than they used to be. They are made of more materials. New metals are being used. Plastic has been invented.

In 1958 people in the United States threw out 70 billion pounds of packages. In 1966 people threw out 103 billion pounds of packages. And by the end of 1976 we will have thrown out about 147 billion pounds of packages. Every year more packages. And every year more pollution.

Convenience Foods

Look at the packages you throw away. You will find that most of them are food packages. Over 43 per cent of all packages are for foods. And many of these foods are "convenience" foods. These are foods that are packaged so that they are very easy to prepare. TV dinners are a good example. They may be convenient, but they cause a lot of waste. First the factory throws away potato skins, boxes, bones, etc. Then you throw away the cardboard box and the metal tray.

PACKAGING POLLUTES

Packaging = Garbage = Pollution

Very few packages are recycled. There are so many kinds of packages that it is hard to collect and separate them.

When we throw packages away, we are harming our environment. Packages pollute the air when they are burned. They use up valuable land when they are buried. They pollute waterways when they get into our lakes and rivers. They make our streets look ugly when they are tossed away as litter. Packages also use up natural resources. A paper bag was once part of a tree, remember.

Litter Problems

What do litterbugs usually litter with? Throwaway bottles. Throwaway cans. Throwaway everything.

When packages are thrown away, they often end up on our streets and sidewalks. Some people did a survey in Kansas. They counted all the litter along a highway. Most of the litter they found was packaging.

Do your own survey. Look closely at litter the next time you see it. How many packages do you see?

Plastic Problems

Some packages pollute more than others. Plastic packages cause many environmental problems. They are very hard to recycle. When they melt in incinerators, they stop up the grates. Some plastics even give off poisonous gases when they are burned.

RETURNABLE BOTTLES

Soda and beer containers are packages. Today people are drinking more beer and soda than ever before. So there are more beer and soda bottles and cans than ever before, too. All of these containers end up as garbage or as litter on our beaches, parks, and streets.

Returnable bottles help to solve some of our garbage and litter problems. Here's how. A returnable bottle is very thick and strong so that it will not break easily. It can be used again and again. When you buy a soda which is in a returnable bottle, you pay an extra amount of money for the bottle. This is called a <u>deposit</u>. The deposit is sometimes two cents or five cents. Sometimes it is more. When you return the empty bottle to the store, the store-keeper gives you your deposit back. (If you don't return your bottle, you lose your deposit, so it pays to bring your bottle back!)

Every few days the soda company picks up the empty bottles that the storekeeper has collected and brings them back to the soda factory. At the factory the bottles are washed and sterilized. Then they are refilled. In this way bottles are used again and again and they don't become garbage for a long time.

Many things used to come in returnable bottles. A very long time ago, people even brought their own containers with them to the dairy farm or store to be filled. Your great grandfather probably had his own pail that he brought to be filled with beer.

But these days a lot of people don't want to be bothered with bringing bottles back to the store. Milk now comes in cartons. Beer and soda come mostly in bottles and cans that say "No Deposit, No Return." These packages may be convenient, but they cause a lot of garbage.

In some states, like Oregon and Vermont, laws have been passed so that beer and soda will only be sold in returnable containers. In those states the people have come to understand that it is wrong to create so much waste. They know that returnable containers help cut down garbage and litter.

You Can Help

1. Buy returnables and return them.
2. Tell others to buy and return returnables.
3. Write to the elected representatives in your state government, and to your senators and congresspeople. Tell them you think returnables are a good idea.
4. Ask stores near you to sell returnables.
5. Write to companies that make soda and beer and tell them to to use returnables.

48

DON'T LET PACKAGES POLLUTE

When you buy returnables, you help solve some of our garbage problems. Be careful when you shop. There are other ways you can keep packages from polluting our environment. Look at packages before you buy things. Ask yourself some questions about the package.

Is the Package Necessary?

Does everything have to come in a package? Of course not. Many things can be stored easily without packages. They won't break. They won't spoil. They are easy to move and carry.

Pens, screwdrivers, spools of thread, miniature cars, hammers. Sometimes you can buy these things without packaging. But other times they are sold in packages called "bubble packs." A "bubble pack" is a piece of cardboard with a plastic bubble over it. The plastic bubble covers the pen, toy, or screwdriver. Is it really necessary? Do things cost more in "bubble packs?"

Nature's "packaging" is very good. Apples, oranges, carrots, and potatoes have skins that protect. But today many stores put packages around the "packages." Do we need them?

Think about all the paper bags you and your family throw away in a year. Years ago people carried their own shopping baskets or cloth bags to stores. They could be used again and again. People still do this today in many foreign countries. They often carry bags made out of string so the bags can fold easily when they are not being used.

Is the Package Made Out of Recycled Materials?

Sometimes packages are made out of recycled materials. Look to see if it says so on the package. But read the label carefully. Learn the difference between recyclable and recycled. Recyclable means it can be recycled. Recycled means it is made out of recycled materials.

Does the Package Waste Materials?

Were you ever disappointed when you opened a box of candy and found a little bit of candy in a great big box? Packages are often bigger than they have to be. A big package sometimes fools people into thinking they are buying more.

Manufacturers waste materials to make fancy packages. They think we will buy their product if it comes in a fancy package. And often we do. Perfume and cosmetics are good examples of pretty over-packaging. Have you ever had this experience? You buy a little bottle of perfume. It comes in a fancy big box. The box is lined with plastic or cardboard. Then it is wrapped with another kind of material. And after that, the salesperson puts the box into a bag for you to carry home.

It is easy to put little cans of pudding in your lunchbox. It is easy to use TV dinners or slices of cheese with paper in between each slice. It is easy and fun to use variety packs of cereal. But these packages waste materials. Add up the amount of cereal in a variety pack. Compare it to the amount of cereal in a big box. Then when you're finished eating, open and measure the boxes. The variety packs use more packaging for the same amount of cereal!

Can the Package Be Recycled?

Some materials are harder to recycle than others. More and more packages are being made out of plastic. Plastic is light. It does not break as easily as glass. But plastic is very hard to recycle. No one wants to do it. Try not to buy things in plastic packages until scientists discover easy ways to recycle plastic.

Packages that are made of more than one material are difficult to recycle, too. The different materials have to be separated first. Have you ever brought bottles to a recycling center? The aluminum caps and rings have to be taken off the bottles before the glass can be recycled. People have been complaining to the bottle companies that it is too hard to recycle bottles with aluminum rings. So the companies have invented twist-off caps that don't leave rings on the bottles. You should complain to companies, too, if their packages are hard to recycle.

CHAPTER SEVEN

Starting a Recycling Center

What do you do in your spare time? Ride a bike? Play baseball? Go to the movies? Lots of people nowadays are breaking bottles, crushing cans, and tying up newspapers in their spare time. Where are they doing this? At recycling centers!

A recycling center is a place where used bottles, cans, and newspapers are collected. These things are then brought to recycling plants where they are made into new bottles, cans, and paper.

Operating a recycling center is hard work. But people in many communities volunteer to do this because they care about the environment. They worry about the pollution that is caused by burning and burying garbage. They worry about wasting the natural resources that are used to make the products we use. They want to see things recycled instead of burned and buried.

Can small recycling centers run by volunteers recycle all the bottles, cans, and paper in our cities? Of course not. But neighborhood recycling centers are important. They make people think about garbage problems. When people find out that garbage doesn't have to be burned or buried, they will tell government officials to build recycling plants in their cities. They will tell companies to make products that can be recycled.

At recycling centers, people also find out that some things are easier to recycle than others. For example, they learn that plastic is difficult to recycle. So they buy glass or metal containers instead. They buy things that are "recyclable" instead of things that have to be thrown away.

Some people learn that they don't have to make so much garbage in the first place. They can buy returnable bottles. They can bring a shopping basket to the store instead of using so many paper bags.

This chapter is for you if you want to know more about recycling centers. It is especially helpful if you and your friends are thinking about starting a recycling center of your own.

WHAT WILL YOU COLLECT AT YOUR CENTER?

Some recycling centers collect just one kind of recyclable material. Others collect many different materials. What you collect depends on how much space you have, how many workers you have, and who will buy your materials.

Paper

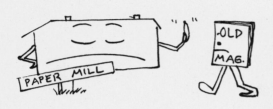

Each paper recycling mill needs a special kind of scrap paper to make recycled paper. Some paper mills are very fussy. Recycling centers have to separate paper for the paper mills. So most recycling centers just collect newspapers. It is easy to separate newspapers from other kinds of paper.

Glass

Many recycling centers collect glass bottles and jars. But bottles must not be mixed with other kinds of glass, like window glass. The bottles and jars also have to be separated by color. Different kinds and colors of glass, like different kinds of paper, can't be recycled together.

Tin-plated Steel Cans

Vegetables and fruits and pet food come in tin-plated steel cans. They are made of steel but they have a coating of tin on the inside. So they are called <u>tin-plated</u>. Magnets will stick to these cans. The side of each can has a seam.

Aluminum

Aluminum is a light metal. A magnet will not stick to it. The bottom of an aluminum can is rounded. You can't see any seam on the sides. Soda and beer often come in these cans. You can also collect aluminum pie tins and TV dinner trays.

Bi-Metal Cans

It is hard to find companies that will recycle bi-metal cans. These cans are made of two different metals. The top is aluminum. The rest of the can is steel. These metals are hard to separate in a recycling plant. The side of each can has a seam.

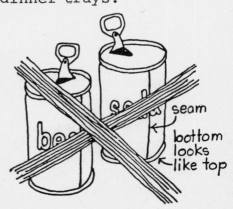

seam

bottom looks like top

52

WHERE WILL YOU PUT EVERYTHING?

Materials have to be put somewhere
while they are being collected. But
where? Newspapers can catch fire easily
if they are stacked and stored for a long
time. The fire department is very fussy
about where they will let people stack
lots of newspapers. Cans pile up pretty
fast. Is there room to save them all?
Glass can be dangerous. Is there a safe
place to store it? Will you collect things
indoors or outdoors? If you collect
outdoors, what will you do when it rains?

If you want to collect
materials in your school, you
will have to get permission
from your principal. He will
want to know what the maintenance
men think. They won't want to
clean up if you make a mess!

WHO WANTS YOUR RECYCLABLES?

Who will buy and recycle the things you
collect? Investigate <u>before</u> you start
collecting. Sometimes the companies that
buy materials for recycling are so far away
that you can't get to them. You don't want
to collect recyclables unless you are sure
you have a place to sell them.

WHO WILL TAKE THEM AWAY?

Most dealers who buy your recyclables will not pick them up.
They don't have the time. They can't afford to pay someone to
drive the truck. So you will have to get them to the dealer yourself. How? Decide <u>before</u> you start collecting. If you don't, you
might be stuck with piles of recyclables and no way to move them.

If you only collect a small amount,
someone with a car might volunteer to help.
Renting a truck costs a lot of money. Can
the school bus be used? Can a community
organization lend you a truck and driver?
Ask around.

These are just a few of the questions
you must ask yourself before you can start
a recycling center. Can you think of more?
We can. Read on.

WHAT HAPPENS AT A RECYCLING CENTER?

Recyclables have to be
processed. This means that certain
things have to be done to them
before they can be recycled.

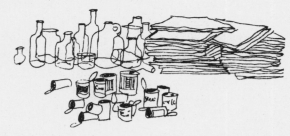

Glass

Many bottles with screw top caps
have metal rings around their necks.
These caps and rings are aluminum. The
caps and rings have to be taken off.
Add them to your aluminum collection.
If the caps are steel, add them to your
steel collection. Bottles and jars also
have to be separated into different
colors--brown, green, and clear.

Many recycling centers break glass
with an electric glass crusher or with
big hammers. They put the glass in
big metal barrels. Crushed glass takes
up much less space.

Cans

Flattened cans take up less space
also. Take the tops and bottoms off
tin-plated steel cans before flattening.
Crush aluminum cans by stepping on them.
Separate tin-plated steel cans from
aluminum cans. Store cans in barrels
or in plastic bags.

Newspaper

Tie newspapers in bundles about twelve
inches high. This way they are easy
to stack and pick up and move.

Who Will Do the Work?

Recycling centers need many workers. Make sure you have
enough volunteers before you open a center. Each volunteer can
do a different job.

- Process materials
- Teach others about recycling
- Pass out leaflets, make posters
- Clean up when the center closes

People should do a lot of processing at home before they bring materials to a recycling center. This will make it easier for the volunteers to get their jobs done.

Here is a sample flyer that many volunteers pass out at recycling centers. It shows people how they should process materials at home.

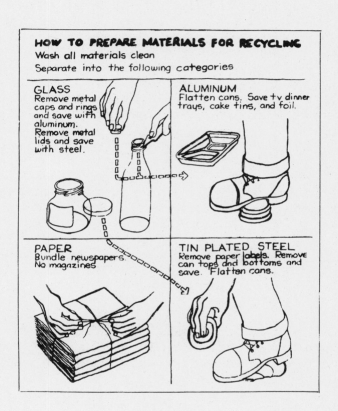

HOW TO PREPARE MATERIALS FOR RECYCLING
Wash all materials clean
Separate into the following categories

GLASS
Remove metal caps and rings and save with aluminum. Remove metal lids and save with steel.

ALUMINUM
Flatten cans. Save tv dinner trays, cake tins, and foil.

PAPER
Bundle newspapers. No magazines

TIN PLATED STEEL
Remove paper labels. Remove can tops and bottoms and save. Flatten cans.

Equipment Check List

You will need some equipment at the recycling center to process the materials that people forget to process at home. You will also need things to help keep your center clean and safe. Use this check list. Have we forgotten anything?

Can openers

Pliers or small knives for removing rings from bottles

Cord and scissors for tying

Protective clothing (gloves, goggles, ear plugs)

Broom or rake

Garbage cans

Bags and/or barrels for collecting recyclables

Supply box

Work table

First Aid kit

MORE THINGS TO THINK ABOUT

When Will Your Center Be Open?

Decide what hours the center will be open. Make sure that volunteers can work during these hours. People should only bring materials when the center is open. What would happen if people left bottles, cans, and paper when the center was closed?

Publicity

No one will come to your recycling center if they don't know about it. Pass out leaflets. Make posters. Put them up in school, in store windows, in apartment buildings. Make buttons for people to wear.

Posters

Form a committee to make posters. Or ask your art teacher if posters can be made in art classes. Remember to put all the important information on your poster:

1. What materials will be collected?
2. When will the center be open?
3. Where is the center located?
4. Who is running the program?

Posters can have other kinds of information also. They can explain how to process materials. They can tell people why it is important to recycle. They can give hints on how to make less garbage.

Displays

Ask for permission to use display cases and bulletin boards in schools, churches and synagogues, and community centers. Put up information about solid waste problems and solutions.

Buttons

Make buttons for kids in school to wear. Try to make them from scrap materials. Ask your art teachers, shop teachers, and home economics teachers for advice.

Special Events

Plan a play, a basketball game, ecology fair, or other event. Instead of money, use a recyclable can or bottle as the price of admission.

Help People Learn About Recycling

Have a volunteer "greet" people when they come into the center. This volunteer can explain how to process materials. He can show people what the different metals look like. He can tell them all about recycling.

Be Careful!

Make your recycling center a safe place to work. Write safety rules for the center. Don't leave glass around where people can break it accidentally. Be careful opening cans. Wear special clothing to protect yourself.

Recycling Centers Have Garbage Problems, Too

How will people carry their recyclables to your center? In bags and boxes, of course. And what will you do with all these bags and boxes when they are empty? You should have a place for people to put this garbage. If you don't, the center will get pretty messy. Remember, you are supposed to be helping the environment, not making a mess!

What Will You Do with the Money You Make?

You have to collect an awful lot of recyclables to make much money. But it is possible. And recycling groups start many different projects with the money they make. Some groups donate the money to charity. Others plant trees. Others buy paint and equipment for clean-ups. Tell people what you will do with the money you make. They might bring more things to your recycling center if they know the money earned is being used for something special and important.

CHAPTER EIGHT

New Life for Old Cars

Every day there are dozens of them
left out in the streets. Cracking, crumbling,
rusting, rotting, and decaying. They fill
up vacant lots and sit on the edges of
superhighways. They make a crowded city
even more crowded. They come in all colors,
shapes, and sizes, but most of them are
old and ugly. What are they? They are
abandoned cars!

You have probably seen abandoned cars in your city. They are
cars that people don't want anymore. Instead of disposing of
them in the right way, these people thoughtlessly just leave them
parked on some street or take them to a vacant lot and leave them
there. Maybe the car is very old and can't be fixed. Maybe
the owner doesn't have the money to fix it. Maybe the owner
just got tired of the old car and wanted to get rid of it quickly.
The car might even be one that was stolen and abandoned when the
thief got tired of it!

Abandoned cars are a real problem. They make our environment
unpleasant. If they are left on the streets too long, they start
to get rusty. The windows get smashed and the cars start to
crumble. It is an ugly sight. Children hurt themselves on
broken glass and pieces of rusty metal. Sometimes rats live in
them. Often they are set on fire. Some cities have special
ways of finding and towing away abandoned cars. But people are
abandoning their cars faster than most cities can get rid of them!

What can people do with their old cars when they don't want
them anymore? What if we managed to get all the abandoned cars
off the streets? What would we do with them? Is there anything
valuable about an old car? Who would want one? These are
questions we are going to answer in this chapter.

USING PARTS OF OLD CARS

Car Transplants

Have you heard about heart transplants and kidney transplants? That's when a part of someone's body wears out and is replaced with a part of someone else's body that's in better condition. The same thing can happen with cars.

Some people have old cars that need tires or batteries or radiators. Maybe they can't afford to buy brand-new parts for these cars. So they go to an automobile junkyard that has lots of old cars. An old car or a car that was in an accident might still have a good battery, or radiator, or tires. It costs much less money to buy these second-hand parts than to buy new ones.

Car and Tire Fun

Have you ever heard of an Adventure Playground? This is a very special kind of playground. The kids get to build their own swings, games, and equipment out of junk.

Old tires are great in Adventure Playgrounds. Kids use tires for all sorts of games. They build swings, obstacle courses, and tunnels. They paint the tires wild colors. Some playgrounds even have whole trucks that don't work anymore for climbing and jumping on.

New Cars from Old Cars

Have you ever seen a car that was built with parts from many different cars? Some of them are very fancy. They don't look like regular cars. Their owners are very proud of them. Sometimes the owners get together to show off their cars. They have contests to see who has the best-looking car.

Learning from Old Cars

There are high schools that teach boys and girls how to become auto mechanics. These students need cars to practice on. People who don't want their cars anymore can bring them to these high schools. They will be put to good use before they go to an automobile junkyard.

RECYCLING PARTS OF CARS

Cars Contain Many Different Metals

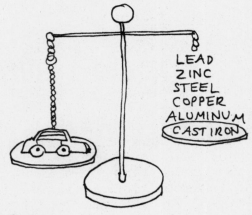

Some people have studied American cars that were built between 1954 and 1965. They discovered that a car that weighed 3,600 pounds contained about 2,500 pounds of steel that could be reused, 500 pounds of cast iron, 32 pounds of copper, 54 pounds of zinc, 51 pounds of aluminum, and 20 pounds of lead. These metals are valuable.

Who Wants These Metals?

These metals can all be recycled. Steel mills will buy back used iron and steel to make more steel. Used copper, zinc, aluminum, and lead auto parts can be sold back to people who will melt them down for other uses. Did you know that more copper and lead is recycled in the United States than is mined here?

Some Parts of Cars Are Hard to Recycle

Add up the weights of all the metals we talked about in a car that weighs 3,600 pounds. Do they add up to 3,600 pounds? What might the rest of the weight be? Seats are not made of metal and they cannot be recycled. Tires are not made of metal and an awful lot of them are not used again. Gas tanks are made of metal but are hard to recycle or resell because they are so dangerous. Carpeting, broken glass, plastic . . . these things are usually useless.

LEARN MORE BY YOURSELF

1. Talk to an auto mechanic or someone who knows a lot about cars. Find out which parts of a car are made of lead, copper, zinc, or aluminum.

2. See if you can find any places where old tires are reused. Can you think of any other uses for old tires?

3. Look in the yellow pages of your telephone book under "Scrap Metals." Call one or two companies and ask what kind of metals they buy. Ask how much they will pay for these metals.

4. Get books from the library about the metals in a car. Where do lead, copper, zinc, and iron come from? How are aluminum and steel made?

AN ABANDONED CAR TAKES A TRIP

The Car

A car gets old. It is abandoned.
A tow truck picks it up and brings it
to an auto wrecker.

The Auto Wrecker

At the auto wrecker's, the car
is "stripped." This means that parts
of the car are taken out. They take
out the parts that can be reused, and
sell them. They take out the parts
that have valuable metals, and sell
them. They take out the parts that no
one wants, and throw them away. Then
the car is sold to a scrap processor.

The Scrap Processor

Scrap processors are people who
make the car ready for recycling. The
car is worth most when the metals are
separated and the things that are not
metal are all removed.

One way to do this is to "shred"
the cars. Have you ever eaten anything
shredded, like shredded coconut or
shredded wheat? Shredding means
tearing into little pieces. The car's
body is shredded into little pieces
by a powerful machine. Then the
different materials are separated
with a magnet. Remember, most of the
metals in a car are steel and iron and
will stick to a magnet.

Steel Mills and Foundries

The scrap processors ship the
steel or iron to steel mills and
foundries. Here the steel and
iron is made into new steel and
iron. The steel and iron is
recycled.

New Products

The final step is to make a
new product from the recycled metals.

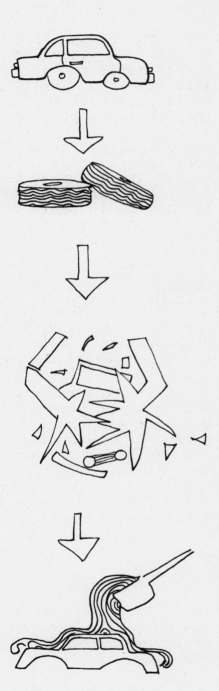

IT'S NOT EASY TO GET RID OF OLD CARS

Why Don't We Recycle More Cars?

If cars can be recycled, why are so many cars abandoned? Why are cars rusting away in automobile junkyards? Why aren't more people rushing to recycle them and earn money?

The reason is that it is hard and expensive for an old car to take the trip from the street to the steel mill. It costs a lot of money to pick cars up and get them ready for recycling. Auto wreckers have to hire men to find the cars and pick them up. It is hard work to "strip" them of their valuable parts and send them to scrap processors and steel mills.

Some people are working to make it easier to recycle cars. They are building more powerful machines like the shredder we talked about. They are working on ways to find cars more quickly and pick them up faster. They are trying to change some laws so it will be less expensive to send scrap metal, by truck and train, to recycling plants.

How Do We Get the Cars Off the Streets?

First we have to teach people not to abandon their old cars and hurt the environment. People should bring their old cars to an auto wrecker if they don't want them anymore. Some cities have a system to pick up your old car for you if you call a special number!

If cars are abandoned by inconsiderate people, they must be picked up by someone else. In some cities the sanitation department picks up abandoned cars. In other cities private companies work with the sanitation department to pick up these cars. Most cities have not solved the problem of abandoned cars very well. Sometimes private citizens get so mad at the mess that they organize abandoned car clean-ups themselves!

LEARN MORE BY YOURSELF

Investigate

1.   Find out how your city gets rid of abandoned cars. Find out how many cars were abandoned last year. Ask someone in city government to talk to your class about this problem. Ask how you can help.

2.   Look in the telephone book under "Automobile Wreckers."
Is there one near your school? Maybe your class can take a trip
to see what happens to cars when they are picked up.

Write

1.   Write to different big cities and ask how they get rid of
old cars. Are any cities doing anything to stop people from
abandoning their cars?

2.   Write to the Institute of Scrap Iron and Steel, Inc., 1729
H Street, N.W., Washington, D.C. 20006 for information about
recycling iron and steel.

3.   The National Association of Recycling Industries (NARI) is
an organization that has a lot of information about recycling.
Write to NARI at 330 Madison Avenue, New York, N.Y. 10017. Ask
about the problems companies have when they try to recycle metals.
Ask about the laws that make it expensive to send old metals to
recycling plants.

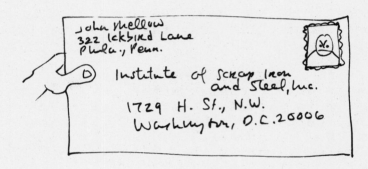

Read

How Do They Get Rid of It? by Suzanne Hilton (The West-
minster Press, Philadelphia). Have you ever wondered what
happens to planes, trains, and ships when they are too old to
be used? Do you know where your garbage and sewage go? Have
you ever seen a building get torn down? This interesting book
tells how people get rid of things when they are not useful any
more. It tells how people got rid of things long ago and how
times have changed.

Some of the things you learn are scary. You see how people
are hurting the environment. Other things are exciting. You
learn how many things can be reused and recycled. There are
pictures of all sorts of mechanical monsters--including the
machines that are used by scrap processors. In fact, there is
a whole chapter about cars and how they can be recycled.

CHAPTER NINE

Caring for Our Cities

Some people have been saying a lot of bad things about cities. Cities are dirty. Cities are noisy. Cities are crowded and unhealthy. And some parts of cities <u>are</u> that way. It's true.

But cities don't have to be unpleasant. People who study what's good and bad about cities say that they can be very good environments for people.

People in cities live close together. So it is often easier to provide the services they need. Garbage can be picked up quicker. Police and fire stations can be located right in the neighborhood. Buses and trains help people travel without using cars that waste lots of energy.

In cities there are always interesting places to visit like museums and movies and big city parks. There are people nearby to share things with. This makes cities exciting and fun.

In New York, the Girl Scouts have been thinking a lot about their city. Like all cities, New York has its problems. But the Girl Scouts decided to help make their city a better place, and we thought it was such a great idea we wanted to share it.

TAKE STOCK IN YOUR CITY

Not long ago the Girl Scouts of New York began taking stock in their city. Each troop met to talk about the city's problems. Their meetings may have sounded like this:

"There's a tree in front of my school," says one Scout, "that was hit by a truck that backed into it. Now some of the bark is peeling off. Trees are beautiful. Cities need trees. People should take better care of them."

"And what about the park around the corner? It would be so nice to play there if people threw their papers and soda cans in the trash baskets instead of on the grass."

"It's air pollution that really bothers me," says one. "Sometimes our air is so polluted, it smells bad and makes my eyes burn. Cars cause air pollution. If we walked or rode our bikes more, the air would be cleaner."

The Girl Scouts found that many of the city's problems could be solved if people cared enough to help. They were glad to be part of "Take Stock in New York." When they completed their projects, they received special patches for the good work they had done.

CITY TREES NEED HELP

Trees make the city more pleasant with their green color and softness. They give cool shade in summer and provide oxygen for the air we breathe. Squirrels, birds, and insects make their homes in city trees.

A Girl Scout troop in Brooklyn, New York, decided their "Take Stock in New York" project would be to care for the street trees in their community. They went on tree walks. They cleaned up the litter around the trees. They loosened the soil so water could get down to the roots. They spread wood chips on the soil of the tree pits to hold moisture, and painted the wound in the bark with special healing paint.

"I feel sorry for trees that nobody takes care of," said one of the Scouts. "So when I go with the Girl Scouts to help the trees, it makes me feel very good. The people from the houses don't mind; they even like it. One time a very nice lady even showed us her plants and gave us seeds. I planted some."

Another reported, "I enjoyed the tree walk because I like to help trees. I really think we did a good job. The trees looked so terrible, but when we got through with them they looked lovely. I'm glad I went on the tree walk even though it was my birthday."

MAKE GREEN SPACES CLEAN SPACES

Parks and other green spaces
are important in cities where
there are so many buildings and
so much gray cement. Green spaces
are like having a little bit of
country right in the middle of
the city.

But many green spaces in the
city are covered with litter.
Benches are often broken. Plants
and trees are neglected.

Many Scout troops in New York turned their attention to
parks, yards, and beaches near their homes. A Junior Troop
in Queens, New York, cleaned out a local churchyard. It was
covered with tree limbs after a terrible ice storm. When the
Scouts were finished, the churchyard could be used again.

Another Troop in Queens spent a whole day cleaning up a
picnic area in a large city park. Many troops in Brooklyn
cleaned up beaches.

Are there any parks, yards, or beaches near your home or
school? Maybe you and your friends can help keep them clean.

MAKE A PARK FROM A VACANT LOT

Here's a big project you
and your friends can do to bring
more green spaces to your city.

Look around your neighborhood
for a neglected vacant lot. Pick
one that needs your help. ASK
GROWN UPS TO HELP YOU. YOU
WILL NEED PERMISSION TO FIX
THE LOT UP.

67

The first job in fixing up the lot will be to clean out all the junk. Your city's Sanitation Department may help you haul the garbage away with their trucks. Pull up the weeds. Dig the soil and plant grass seed. Plant a flower garden or vegetables. Then play or relax and enjoy the beautiful space you've made.

CLEAN, CLEAN WATER

Even in cities there are ponds, lakes, and streams. If you have a little body of water near your home or school, check it out. Is it clean or dirty? Is the water clear and beautiful? Or is it full of cans, bottles, and paper?

Girl Scout troops in Bayside, Queens, decided to care for a neglected body of water in their area called Oakland Lake. The space around the lake had been rebuilt by the city. But thoughtless people kept littering it.

The Scouts contacted the Parks Department. They told them they wanted to clean up Oakland Lake. The people at the Parks Department thought it was a great idea! They supplied all the tools the Scouts needed to do the job. The girls hauled garbage out of the water, picked up litter from the trails, and planted flowers all around.

A group of grown ups in the community was so pleased with the Scouts' job that each girl was given a certificate saying "Congratulations!" Oakland Lake is now a much healthier and prettier place.

CITY STREETS CAN BE BEAUTIFUL

If you live in the city, you probably spend more of your time on sidewalks and streets than you do at beaches and parks. The city street is the environment that is closest to city people.

One Girl Scout Troop in Queens did a street clean-up for their "Take Stock in New York" project. They spent a Saturday morning making the largest street in their community neat and tidy. Using plastic litter bags, shovels, and brooms, they turned their street into a clean and pleasant place for walking and shopping.

"We started from the church with our brushes and brooms," said one Scout. "We got lots of bottles and junk. We spent hours cleaning up. I never saw so much garbage in my life!"

Testing Your Street

Pick a street near your home or school and give it a test. Here are some questions you can ask. Think of some others, too.

1. Are the sidewalks and gutters clean?

2. Are there litter containers at the corners?

3. Are there enough tightly covered garbage cans for each building?

4. Are there trees on the block? Are they well-cared for?

5. Are vacant lots clean and attractive?

If there are a lot of "yes" answers on your street's test, yours is a Super Street. If there are lots of "no" answers, why not plan a street clean-up soon?

"BIKE-AWAY"

Cars cause air pollution. They waste energy and make city streets unsafe, crowded, and noisy.

The Girl Scouts of New York held a "Bike-Away" to show how using bikes instead of cars can help the city. There were bike parades, poster contests, bike hikes, and demonstrations on bicycle safety. The Scouts also registered their bikes with the Police Department so that if a bike were ever stolen, it would be easier to locate.

From these activities, Scouts learned that biking is good exercise, and fun to do. It is a clean form of transportation. It takes you where you want to go quickly and quietly. And it's great to bike with the whole family.

A Girl Scout from Queens said, "Our troop had a 'bike-away' in the park. We all got stickers and booklets on how to take care of our bicycles. I like biking better than riding a car. Riding my bicycle is quiet and it does not pollute the air. I also can see more things when I ride. I had such a good time!"

CHAPTER TEN

People and Our Earth

How many people are in your classroom? How many books, chairs, desks, and paper supplies are there? Have you ever invited another class into your room? What happened? Did it get hotter? Noisier? Was it more fun? Did you have enough chairs and desks? What if you were more daring? What if you invited still another class into your room? Now there would be three classes in a room usually used by just one class!

In a way, your classroom is like the earth. There is only so much space. The room can't get bigger. It can hold only so many chairs. There are only so many pencils, papers, and books. And there are many students who all want to use those limited supplies.

You might say, "If it gets too crowded, we can always move to the auditorium." That's true. But can we say, "When the earth gets too crowded, we can always move to Mars?" Today there are 3 billion people on earth. That's the earth's population. In 30 years there may be 7 billion people. In 30 years you may have children in school. What will life on earth be like then?

Mr. Laurence Pringle wrote a book for young people about population problems. He called it One Earth, Many People. Do you see why he chose this title? He is worried because the number of people on earth is growing, but the earth is not. People take up space on earth. They need things like food and clothes. Will there be enough space, food, natural resources, and energy for people to live well in the future? Will more people cause more pollution?

One thing is true. The earth is only so big. It has only so much water, land, and resources. We have to be sure that the number of people fits the earth so that all people can live healthy, comfortable lives. This takes planning. It takes learning about how people live. Think about it. Just how many people are too many people?

PEOPLE.   PEOPLE.   AN AWFUL LOT OF PEOPLE!

People Like Living Near Each Other. . .

        People like to be close. We like to have
friends and share things. We want to visit and
talk to one another. Children like to play
together. We feel special when we are with
family and friends.

. . . but People Do Not Like Being Crowded

        People do not like to live too close
together. When we do, we feel crowded.
Crowding makes some people want to push.
We get angry. There's not always enough
room to play in a crowded city. Crowds are
noisy. Buses and streets get dirtier when
too many people are using them.

        It's hard to feel special when there
are too many people. Nobody wants to be
alone. But we don't want to get squashed
either!

Some People Are Trying to Slow Down Population Growth

        Some parents have decided that they and their children will
have better lives if they have small families. They don't want
their children to live in a crowded world. They worry about all
the new houses, hospitals, schools, colleges, and parks that
will have to be built if the population keeps growing.

        Some people have formed organizations to teach others about
over-population and the problems it brings. One of these groups
is called Zero Population Growth--ZPG for short. ZPG says that if
most people have small families, the world may some day reach
"zero population growth." This means that the number of people
who are born each year will equal the number of people who die.
So the population will stay the same. It won't grow. For this
to happen, each family would have to have no more than two children.

        Here's a letter from a young boy who is troubled by the
population problem.

Dear Zero Population Growth,

I think there are too many people in our city.
Last year we went camping. All the animals left the
park because there were too many people and too much
noise. My mother says you are telling people to have
only 2 children. What can I do? I am only in the
third grade.
Sincerely,
A Friend

People Are Consumers

Food. Clothes. Furniture. These are goods that people
use. This is called consuming. People consume. Buses, schools,
hospitals. These are services. They serve our need to go
places, to learn, to be healthy. People consume services as well
as goods.

What do all of these things have in common? They use
up resources from the earth. They use trees, plants, land. They
use metals and fuels. They also cause some pollution. Remember
how power plants cause air pollution and packages cause garbage?

The more people there are, the more goods and services
we need. This means we will be taking more resources from the
earth and we will be causing more pollution.

PEOPLE PROJECTS

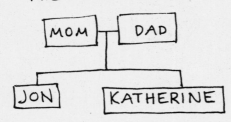

THE SMITH FAMILY

Draw a Family Tree

Have you ever drawn a family tree?
This is a chart that shows how a family
grows in size. It is also a way of seeing
how fast the population can grow.

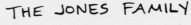
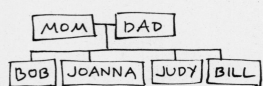

THE JONES FAMILY

Here we have drawn family trees
for two imaginary families. Which
family contributes more to population
growth? Which family is helping to
slow down population growth? Draw
your own family tree. Compare it
with the ones on this page.

Do Some Figuring

1.   What if each child in the Jones family got married and had
two children?

*How many people would be in the Jones family then?
*How many new houses would have to be built for them to live in
 with their new families?

2.   What if each child in the Smith family got married and had
four children?

*How many people would be in the Smith family then?
*How many new houses or apartments would have to be built for
 them to live in with their new families?

3.   Look at the family tree you have drawn of your family.
How many children do you think you and your brothers and sisters
will have if you get married?

*How many people would be in your family then?
*How many new houses or apartments would have to be built for you
 to live in with your new families?

Use Your Imagination

Think about what life might be like in the year 2000 if
population continues to grow as fast as it is growing now. Write
a story or play about it.

Investigate

Find out about population growth in different countries.
Where is the population growing the fastest? Where is it slowing
down? Why do you think the numbers of people are growing faster
in some countries than in others?

WHAT DO YOU THINK?

Are there population problems where you live? How can you tell? What can you look for? We'll give you some ideas on this page. Think of some others.

1.   Is there always room for you to sit on the bus? Does crowding make the bus driver yell at people?

2.   What is it like to shop in the stores near you? Does crowding make people shove and act nasty to others?

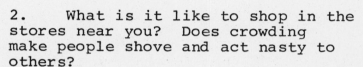

3.   Is your father often late for work because of traffic jams?

4.   Are there places big enough to play baseball where you live? Can you skate fast in your neighborhood?

5.   Are elevators ever too full for you to get in?

6.   Are there schools near you on double session? Are your classrooms very crowded?

7.   Make a list of "signs" of over-population. Put them on a chart like the one below. Record the number of times you see or experience each "sign" each day of the week.

Signs	S	M	T	W	T	F	S
1. Traffic jam.							
2. No seat on the bus.							
3. Waiting in line at the movies.							
4.							
5.							
6.							

LEARN MORE ABOUT POPULATION PROBLEMS

Write

Zero Population Growth (ZPG). Ask them for information on population growth. Their address is 50 West 40th Street, New York, New York 10018.

Read

One Earth, Many People by Laurence Pringle (The Macmillan Company, New York).

The Little House by Virginia Lee Burton (Houghton Mifflin Company, Boston). Mrs. Burton tells a story about a house that changes as more and more people come to live in the town. It is a sad story. Read it to a younger brother or sister.

Sing

Tweedles and Foodles for Young Noodles. This is a book of songs about population. It was written for kids by a 70-year-old woman in California named Melvina Reynolds. Write to Schroeder Music, 2027 Parker Street, Berkeley, California 90247.

CHAPTER ELEVEN

The City's Forest

Close your eyes for a minute and think about TREES.

What did you see? Big trees? Little trees? A forest full of tall trees, or one lonely, skinny, short tree? Short, round trees with branches loaded with juicy red apples? Christmas trees? Big oak trees with many leafy branches? Droopy weeping willows?

If people all over the world closed their eyes this minute and thought about trees, they would all imagine different trees. One of the reasons trees are so interesting to learn about is that they are all so different. Some trees need a lot of soil because they have big sprawling roots. These grow best in the country, where there is room for them to grow. Some trees need lots of water. Willow trees do. They can't grow in the desert. But desert palms don't mind dryness at all. They don't need a lot of water to live. Some trees need a lot of sunlight while others can grow very well with just a little sunlight. There are all kinds of trees in the world because the environment is different in each place that trees grow.

Trees have special problems in cities. There isn't much room for their roots to spread out. Trees that need lots of sunlight don't grow well near tall buildings that block out the sun. Air pollution from cars, trucks, buses, and factories can kill weak trees. But some trees get used to city life.

This chapter is about city trees and how special they are. We'll tell you how trees help improve the environment of a city. You'll also learn about many problems that trees have when they grow in a city environment.

77

CITY TREES HELP US IN MANY WAYS

Trees Share

Trees are like hotels for many living things. Trees in city parks and on the empty land next to highways share their berries, nuts, and seeds with birds and small animals. They let birds, squirrels, and insects use their branches, trunks, roots, and leaves for homes.

Trees Are Nice to Look At

People can get very tired of looking at cement sidewalks, brick buildings, and paved streets. Cement and brick seem cold and unfriendly. They are boring. Cities without trees can be ugly, dull places to look at and live in. Ugliness is pollution just like air pollution and water pollution. It is pollution you can see.

Trees Make Us More Comfortable in Hot Weather

What's life in the city like on a hot summer day? Do you ever want to escape the heat? Which would you rather do on a hot day, sit on a curb outside an apartment house or sit under a tree?

The air under a tree is cooler than the air where there are no trees. Trees give shade and protection from the sun. Trees also act like air conditioners in the heat. Roots send water from the soil to the leaves. Water in the leaves evaporates in the hot weather. The evaporated water helps to keep the air around a tree moist and cool.

Big trees with lots of leaves will evaporate more water than little trees with few leaves. A big elm tree on a hot summer day might give off as much as 7 tons of water! It would make as much cool air as 10 room air conditioners that are running for 20 hours.

Cool air is heavier than hot air. This cool air from the shade and the evaporated water sinks to the ground. It pushes up the warm air. All this movement of air causes breezes. Breezes make you more comfortable on a hot summer day.

Trees Help Save Our Soil

Rain sometimes washes away good soil that plants need to grow. Tree roots hold onto the soil. Leaves help protect the soil, too. Big raindrops hit the leaves and break up into smaller drops that won't disturb the soil when they hit it.

Trees Are Oxygen Producers

We all need oxygen to live. We breathe
in oxygen from the air and breathe out a
gas called carbon dioxide. But where does
the oxygen we breathe come from? Why hasn't
it all been used up by now? The answer is that
trees and other green plants keep putting
oxygen into the air. They take carbon dioxide
out of the air when they make their food.
Then they put oxygen back into the air for us
to breathe.

Trees Help Fight Pollution

City air is dirty air. Think about all the cars, trucks,
and buses in a city. Think about all the factories and incinerators that put dirt and gases into the air. Air pollution
hurts trees as well as people. But trees also help protect
us from the dirt and gases in the air. Trees help make the air
a little cleaner. How do they do this?

Leaves on trees catch some of the dirt in the air. When
it rains, the dirt is washed off the leaves and returned to
the ground. And remember that trees are putting fresh oxygen
into the air every day. They do this through their leaves, too.

Trees can even help fight noise pollution. You can escape many city noises
when you go to a big city park where there
are lots of trees. A street with many
trees is quieter than a street with few
trees. The trees seem to soak up noises
just the way a sponge soaks up water.

Superhighways are noisy places.
Trees and shrubs that are planted close
together along highways act like a
barrier to the sound waves. People who
live next to highways will not be as
bothered by noisy cars and trucks if
there are trees nearby.

Trees Are Nice to Live With

Trees make our neighborhoods nicer
places to live in. The air smells
fresher in places that have a lot of
trees. Somehow people feel happier
when they are near things that are
pretty.

Visit a small park where people
sit under the trees to rest and talk
together. Do the people seem friendlier
and more relaxed?

CITY TREES HAVE SPECIAL PROBLEMS

Trees Need Light

Trees need sunlight to make food for themselves. Tall buildings in the city can block the sunlight from a tree. Sometimes trees in the city grow in funny directions, instead of straight up, because they are trying to reach the sunlight.

Trees Need Soil

It's hard for tree roots to grow when the tree is surrounded by cement. Some trees have roots that spread out near the top of the soil and crack the cement.

Sometimes the cement around a tree acts like an oven and holds in the heat of the day. The roots can bake in the heat. Some city trees get burned very badly in the summer.

When trees are planted, they are often put in holes that are too small. The roots are crushed and pushed against the trunk of the tree. The tree trunk gets fatter and bigger and so do the roots. But the roots have no place to grow except against the trunk. They end up strangling the tree.

Trees Need Air

Trees need clean air to live. Trees help us by taking some pollution gases out of the air, but too much air pollution can make trees sick. Some trees are stronger than others, but trees are hurt by polluted air just the way people are. In fact, one way we can tell how bad air pollution is getting is by watching how it damages the trees, bushes, and flowers in our cities.

Trees Need Water

Trees can get pretty thirsty in a city. If the soil around a tree is very hard and packed down, water will not be able to get to the roots. It will stay at the top of the soil and then evaporate. To find water, the roots will have to grow up instead of down.

Sometimes water has trouble reaching the soil. Look up at a tree. Branches of a tree act like an umbrella. Water splashes off the leaves onto the ground. But if the branches go out over the sidewalk, the water splashes onto the cement. It can't get into the soil and down to the roots.

Trees Need Protection from Salt

When it snows, salt is usually put
on city streets to melt the snow. Cars
splash the salty water on the trees and
on the soil around the trees. People
sprinkle salt on the sidewalks, too.
The melting snow and salt go into the
soil. All this salt can hurt trees,
expecially newly planted trees that
are not very strong.

Trees Need Protection from Animals

People often let their dogs use trees and
the area around them as bathrooms. This hurts
the trees and could even kill them. Some
people put fences around trees to keep the dogs
away. Years ago trees used to have very high
shields around them because people would hook
their horse chains around the tree. In those
days trees had a problem they don't have today.
Sometimes the horses would chew their bark off!

Trees Need People Who Care

Trees have all sorts of people problems.
They are often hurt by thoughtless people.
Sometimes people carve into the bark.
People litter around the trees. Sometimes
they break off branches just for fun when they
are walking along. Drivers carelessly back
their cars into trees when they are parking.

Remember that a tree is alive. Bark
protects a tree just like your skin protects you. But when you cut into a tree,
you are wounding it. These wounds might
get infected and the tree could die.

Even playful things like walking
along and jumping up to grab a leaf from
a branch can harm a tree. Think about
all the things we said leaves do for us.
Leaves give us oxygen. They catch dirt
in the air. Trees need their leaves, and
so do we.

CITY TREES NEED YOUR HELP

The Bedford-Stuyvesant Tree Corps is a group of boys and girls that takes care of the trees in their neighborhood. Of course they have to learn a lot about trees first. They go to classes three times a week to study gardening and tree care. They watch slides and movies. They do experiments.

Then they go out with their teacher and help take care of the trees in their community. They study each tree to decide what kind of help it needs. They look at each part of the tree. Does it need water? Is the soil too hard? Does it look sick? Sometimes they decide that a sick tree needs expert help and they call the Parks Department.

You can help take care of city trees, too. A good book to help you is <u>Caring for Trees on City Streets</u> by Joan Edwards for the Environmental Action Coalition (Charles Scribner's Sons, 1975). There is information about how trees are beneficial to cities, and there are lots of photographs and suggestions on how to select and care for city trees.

Give a Tree a Drink of Water

If it has not rained for several days, city trees will be thirsty. They get especially thirsty in the spring and summer. You can help. Pour a <u>few buckets</u> of water on the dirt around the tree. But don't use too much water. Water the tree until puddles start to form on the top of the soil and then stop watering.

You can use a hose to water trees. But you must be very careful. Turn it on <u>gently</u>, so that the water is running only a little. Then put the hose nozzle down into the tree pit. Let it stay there for about half an hour.

Loosen the Soil

You can help the water get down to the roots by loosening the soil around a tree whenever it gets hard. You must be very careful when you do this. Only break up the top 2 inches of soil around the tree. If you go down more than 2 inches, you might hurt the roots. What kind of tool could you use to safely loosen the soil?

Defend Trees--They're Your Friends

Don't let people wound trees by breaking branches or carving on them. Don't let them pour oil, gasoline, detergents, or other harmful liquids on the soil around the tree. Tell everyone how important healthy trees are to people.

Wash Away That Salt

You can protect a tree from the salt that is put on sidewalks and streets to melt snow. Take buckets of water and throw the water at the soil under the tree so the salt is washed onto the street.

Tell people who put salt on the sidewalks that it would be better to melt the snow and ice with sodium chloride or sand. Sodium chloride is more expensive than salt, but it will not hurt the trees the way salt does.

Don't Litter

Trees are pretty. Garbage is ugly. Garbage can also hurt trees. When litter is thrown on the soil around the trees, it keeps water from reaching the roots.

Don't litter. Clean up the litter that people throw on the ground around trees.

Keep Dogs Away from Street Trees

Don't let dogs use trees as bathrooms. Explain to dog owners that the bark and roots of trees are injured this way. Show them sections of dead bark at the base of injured trees. Tell them to bring their dogs to the curb.

Some block associations have put signs on the trees on their street to remind people about this problem. One sign used in New York City says:

> Dogs don't disturb
> if led to the curb.

Make up your own signs and tie them around trees. Don't use staples or nails that will harm the bark. Maybe your class can earn some money to put up little fences around trees near your school so dogs won't be able to reach them.

Get Special Help for Sick Trees

Trees sometimes have problems that you can't solve by yourself. They might have broken or dead branches that can get infected. They need protection from harmful insects and diseases. Some trees with diseases should be removed before they give these diseases to other trees.

Study the trees where you live. Do any of them have broken branches, holes, or leaves that are curly, chewed up, or falling off? If they do, they need someone to help them who is especially trained to take care of sick city trees. Call the Parks Department in your city and ask them to help.

Adopt a Tree

Adopt a tree near your home or school. Learn about it. Study it. Water it when it is thirsty. Protect it from animals and people who don't care. Call the Parks Department if it is sick or damaged. Remember, the people whose job it is to take care of trees in your city don't have time to watch over all the trees all the time. If you don't care for trees, who will?

HELP MAKE OUR CITIES GREENER--

PLANT A TREE

Cities Need More Trees

People are getting tired of cities
without trees. They want pretty trees
to make the cement buildings more pleasant.
They want trees with berries and nuts that
will attract birds and small animals. They
want little parks where they can sit in
the shade and relax.

What Trees Grow Best in Our Cities?

Not all city environments are alike.
Trees that grow well in one city may not grow
well somewhere else. Some cities have more
air pollution than other cities.

Trees that grow well in one neighborhood
might die many blocks away. For example, some
neighborhoods have many skyscrapers that block
out the sunlight. Other neighborhoods have
smaller buildings with sunny backyards where
trees grow well.

City environments can change. Trees that were healthy in
a city years ago might be dying today. People in Tokyo, Japan,
for instance, are very worried about their beautiful Japanese
flowering cherry trees. There used to be many of these trees in
Tokyo. But now they are dying. There are more factories and
cars in Tokyo now and the pollution is killing the cherry trees.

You Need Help to Plant a Tree

These days many people are planting trees
in their neighborhoods. But this is not an
easy thing to do. It takes a lot of study to
decide what trees will grow best in each city
and in each neighborhood. You need advice
from a tree expert.

Trees cost money. Who will pay for them? Where will you
plant them? You must get permission to plant the tree if it
will be on city property. And who will do the work? If a tree
is not planted properly, it may die. Trees should be planted
carefully by tree experts. And remember, trees also have to be
cared for after they are planted. There are organizations that
will help you plant city trees. Find out who they are and contact
them when you are ready to plant.

EXPLORE THE "LUNGS OF THE CITY"

If you live in a big city or visit one some time, you can discover and explore the "lungs of the city." Of course, cities don't really have lungs! But there are special parts of cities that scientists and environmentalists are beginning to call "lungs."

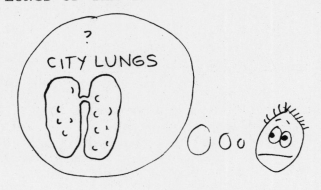

Have you guessed what these "lungs" are? They are the huge parks that can be found in some cities. Some of the parks are very famous, such as Central Park in New York City and Golden Gate Park in San Francisco. These enormous, fresh, green spaces make it possible for people to live in locations where stone, concrete, and asphalt have covered most of the land.

While you are exploring the parks, take a "tree walk." First, go to the library for a picture book on trees that grow in your city's parks. Study the pictures carefully. Then go to the park and try to match the leaves on the park trees with the pictures you have seen. This way you will begin to learn the names of the trees you observe. After you have identified the trees, go back to your book for more fascinating information about each of them.

Here's another good idea. Write to the Parks Council in New York City for their "Tree Table." This is a tiny pocket-size guide to trees that grow in many city parks. You will be able to take the "Tree Table" with you when you go on your tree walk. Send 10 cents to The Parks Council at 80 Central Park West, New York, New York 10023.

86

CHAPTER TWELVE

Birds in the City

Birds are found almost everywhere in the world. But different birds like different environments. Some birds like hot weather. Others enjoy cold weather. Some birds like the seashore. Others prefer our lakes and streams. Some birds like the peace and quiet of the countryside. And still others like the hustle and bustle of cities. There are different birds everywhere you go.

All birds need four things to live. They need food, water, protection from their enemies, and places to build their nests. But what kind of food? How much water? What enemies? And what kinds of nests? Birds choose environments that have just the right food, water, protection, and nesting places for them.

Like trees, birds have special problems in cities. Cities are crowded and noisy. Most birds want to nest where there are more trees and shrubs and supplies of food and water. They want to be where nature protects them. Where can birds hide from their enemies among all those tall, concrete buildings?

But some birds love city life. They don't mind the noise or the buildings. They enjoy living near people. And they like to eat the food we throw away. There are four kinds of birds that live in almost all cities. They are <u>sparrows</u>, <u>pigeons</u>, <u>gulls</u>, and <u>starlings</u>.

We see many other birds in cities too. There are more than 200 different kinds of birds in New York City alone! Most of these birds live in city parks, backyards, vacant lots, and other places that remind them of their favorite environments. But sparrows, pigeons, gulls, and starlings live right among the streets and buildings.

LEARNING TO LIVE IN CITIES

The colonists found many native birds
when they came to this country. But as cities
grew, birds started to fly away. Trees were
cut down to make room for buildings and roads.
Food and nesting places disappeared. Where
can birds find worms, wild fruit, insects,
or nuts to eat in a city? How many trees and
bushes are there? Do you see why many birds
move away from cities?

Some birds changed as the cities
changed. They adapted to city life.
This means that they learned to fit into
a place they weren't used to. You are
adaptable if you can change when things
around you change.

Birds adapted to city life in
different ways. They learned to eat food
from people. They moved into parks and
backyards. They discovered birdfeeders
and birdbaths. They found new places to
build their nests. Have you ever seen
bird nests in abandoned cars or under roofs?

Most birds just visit cities in
certain seasons. Some live in our
parks and backyards for a while.
Then they go away during the cold
weather or when they want to raise
a family. Others just stop to eat
and rest in cities during a long
trip. And some lucky birds find
homes in special places set aside
for them by city people. In these
wildlife sanctuaries, birds are
protected from city life.

The birds that like the city best were
brought here from Europe many years ago. Pigeons,
sparrows, and starlings lived with man in European
cities. But even these birds changed as cities
changed. House sparrows used to eat the seeds
in horse droppings on city streets. But we use
cars now, instead of horses, so sparrows have
learned to eat other foods.

More birds will visit our cities if we help them adapt to
city life and provide more places for them to live. Build a bird-
house or put out a birdbath. Plant trees and shrubs. Tell people
we need more parks, botanical gardens, and wildlife sanctuaries
in our cities.

CITY LIVING ISN'T EASY FOR BIRDS

Insecticides

Trees in cities often have to be sprayed to kill harmful insects. This is because there aren't enough natural enemies, like birds, to eat the insects. But these insecticides can hurt the birds that are left. They can poison the food birds eat and the water they drink.

Water Pollution

In cities there are many factories that use chemicals. The factories sometimes dump their waste chemicals into rivers when they are done with them. Spilling chemicals into rivers poisons the fish some birds eat, and the birds may die.

Air Pollution

As we know, cities have big air pollution problems. The dirt from air pollution settles in the water birds drink, and may make them sick. Polluted air affects birds in some very strange ways. For example, hawks can't glide in air that's too polluted because pollution makes air heavy. Hawks need lightweight air in order to rise.

Bright Lights

Brightly lit skyscrapers cause the death of many birds that migrate at night. The strong lights confuse the birds as they are flying and they sometimes crash into the buildings and die. In New York City, the Empire State Building and the Tishman Building turn off their lights at night during the birds' migrating season. They started doing this in 1961 because so many **birds** were killed crashing into the buildings.

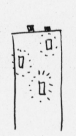

Disappearing Marshes

When cities get bigger, more land is needed for roads and buildings, and disposing of garbage. Marshes are sometimes drained to make room for landfills and for new buildings. But many birds live in marshes. And draining marshes means that birds have fewer places to live and less food to eat.

BIRDS HELP OUR ENVIRONMENT

Birds Protect Plants from Harmful Insects

Birds help trees and other plants by eating harmful insects. This "balance of nature" is very important because when there are not enough birds to eat the harmful insects, the insect population gets bigger and bigger. Too many insects may cause trees and plants to get sick and die.

Over a hundred years ago, New York City's balance of nature was upset. We have learned that as cities grow, many birds fly away to places with more trees and plants. New York City had an invasion of caterpillars because so many birds had flown away from the city. The caterpillars went from tree to tree eating up all the leaves. As people walked under the trees, caterpillars kept falling on their heads. There was nothing to stop the insects because their natural enemies, the birds, were disappearing from the city.

What New York City needed were birds that ate insects and liked living in the city. Cities in Europe already had birds like this. House sparrows had been living happily in European cities for many years. These birds ate insects as well as grain. Over a hundred house sparrows were brought to New York City from England. Some died, but many lived and had families. The house sparrows were so successful in getting rid of the caterpillars that other cities brought sparrows from Europe also. Soon there were house sparrows in cities all across the United States.

Some Birds Help Clean Up Our Cities

City litter is food for some city birds. They eat left-overs from city streets and from garbage cans. Gulls help keep our rivers and harbors clean by eating dead fish and litter.

Birds Make New Plants Grow

Birds make new plants grow by spreading seeds. They eat fruits from trees and drop the seeds near the places where they perch. Other seeds stick to the birds' feathers and are carried to new places as the birds fly. Seeds are even carried in the mud that sticks to the birds' feet. As many as 82 plants have been grown from the mud taken from a bird's foot.

City birds have a hard time making plants grow in the city because there is concrete everywhere. When they drop seeds on city streets, plants can't grow because there is no soil. The little green plants and trees growing out of cracks in sidewalks have a hard time staying alive. More parks are needed in cities so that birds can drop seeds on the soil. Then new plants will grow.

Birds Are Nice to Look At

Birds are beautiful. Think of all the pretty colors and patterns you see on birds' bodies. There are speckles or stripes of brown and white, bright reds and blues. Think of the long slender legs and beaks some birds have. Notice the flight of birds as they swoop gracefully through the air. Look at the funny walk of pigeons, bobbing their heads as they go, and the waddle of ducks in the parks. Birds make dull, gray city places bright and beautiful.

Birds Sing Sweet Songs

City people get so tired of the same old loud noises--subways screeching, horns honking, radios blaring. It is nice to hear the cheerful chirping of birds among the other sounds of the city.

FOUR BIRDS THAT LOVE CITY LIFE

House Sparrows

These little brown birds live easily in cities because they are adaptable. Sheltered places like holes in trees and buildings or ivy on a wall are good nesting places for house sparrows. They use almost anything they can find to make their nests. They eat insects, seeds, and grain. But they also eat some foods we throw away. House sparrows live well in hot or cold weather. So they can stay in the city all year round.

It's a good thing that sparrows aren't fussy eaters because they have large families to feed. They are very social. They build their nests close together and travel in groups.

House sparrows are good city birds, but they do cause some problems. Groups of them can be very noisy. Sparrows are also greedy and mean to other birds. They chase birds away from nesting and feeding places.

Starlings

Starlings don't look very pretty from far away. But up close you can see their shiny black feathers reflecting green and purple colors. In the spring and summer their pointy bills are yellow. Starlings fool people. They can imitate the sounds of over 60 different birds.

Starlings and sparrows are alike in many ways. Starlings travel in groups. They drive other birds away from their nests and feeding places. Starlings have large families and like to nest in sheltered places.

Starlings eat mostly insects and other small animals. So they often fly to the suburbs in the morning to get food and then return to the city to sleep. Unlike sparrows, starlings migrate during certain seasons.

Starlings like to perch together on city buildings and statues. But their droppings stain everything. They also throw up their food a lot. This can make buildings and statues smelly and messy.

Pigeons

Many years ago the colonists brought pigeons with them for food. The wild pigeons we see on city streets today are descendants of these pigeons from Europe.

City pigeons cause a lot of arguments. Some people love them. They are pretty and fun to watch. Their cooing is nice to listen to. People like to feed them in the park or put food out for them on window ledges or fire escapes. But other people say that rats are attracted to the food left over from feeding pigeons. They get angry when they see the mess pigeons make with their droppings. They think pigeons are dirty and that their droppings cause disease.

City pigeons like to make their nests in old buildings that have lots of little corners and places to hide in. Pigeons, sparrows, and starlings hate new skyscrapers because they are usually flat and have no hiding places!

Pigeons depend on the food people give them. They stay in the city all year but they often starve in the winter because people don't like to stay out in the cold just to feed pigeons. Pigeons need lots of water. That is why you see them under dripping air conditioners in the summer and near steam pipes that melt snow and ice in the winter.

Herring Gulls

When the settlers arrived in America, the first birds they saw were the herring gulls. These birds came out to meet the ships and ate the scraps of food thrown overboard for them.

Unlike many of the native birds who flew away from cities, herring gulls enjoyed having people as neighbors. Gulls eat fish. Gulls are also <u>scavengers</u>. They eat things that people throw away. They find lots of food in garbage dumps, in sewage outlets, or on littered beaches.

Gulls usually live near salt water, but they also live near lakes and rivers. It is fun to watch gulls flying gracefully overhead. Their long wings help them soar high in the sky and dip down toward earth again. In cities, the air moves upwards from the streets lined with tall buildings. Gulls can use this moving air to fly easily and beautifully over cities.

HELP CITY BIRDS SURVIVE

MAKE A BIRD FEEDER

One big problem for city birds is finding enough food to eat. You can help birds find food when you put out a bird feeder. You can make a bird feeder yourself.

Most birds like to eat sunflower seeds and wild bird seed. Fill your bird feeder with seeds. Then hang it in a tree in a small park, on the school grounds, or in your backyard.

Make a feeder that doesn't have a perch. Make it with small openings so squirrels, rats, and other animals can't get in and steal the food.

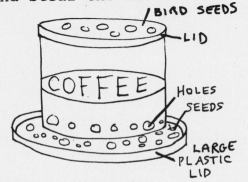

Here's one kind of bird feeder you can make. This one was designed by fifth graders at Seminary Hill School in West Lebanon, New Hampshire. They used scrap materials to make their feeder so it didn't cost any money.

1. Place a coffee can on a plastic lid. The lid should be larger than the can.

2. Drive large nail holes along bottom rim of can.

3. Fill can from the top with bird seed.

4. Cover top of can tightly with the plastic lid that comes with the coffee can.

5. Bird seed will gradually spill out onto the edges of the big lid at the bottom.

6. When can is empty, fill again from the top.

94

LEARN MORE BY YOURSELF

Read

Birds in the Street: The City Pigeon Book by Winifred and Cecil Lubell (Parents' Magazine Press, New York). This interesting book will tell you all about pigeons and how they live. Did you know that pigeons eat about one pound of food a week? Read this book and find out more.

House Sparrows: Ragamuffins of the City by J. J. McCoy (The Seabury Press, New York). Are house sparrows pests? Are they useful birds? Some people think that house sparrows should be driven out of cities. But Mr. McCoy loves sparrows. He thinks they are useful birds who have been treated unfairly by many city people.

Write

The National Audubon Society has been working to protect our environment. They know a lot about birds and how they live. Write to them and ask about birds where you live. Write to: National Audubon Society, 950 Third Ave., New York, N.Y. 10007.

CHAPTER THIRTEEN

Butterfly Season

Almost everyone has seen butterflies. On a sunny day they are hard to miss. Did you ever wonder why we call these beautiful creatures butterflies? Some of them have deep yellow wings, just like the color of butter. Maybe that is how they got their name. But no one is really sure.

Butterflies can be very mysterious. People have always wondered what they were. Long ago, some people thought that butterflies were wandering spirits. Others believed that they were signs of good luck.

Have you ever looked closely at a butterfly? Most of what we know about them has come from careful observation. If you look, you will see that they have four wings and six legs. Their bodies are divided into three parts--a head, a middle (thorax), and an end (abdomen). This means that butterflies are insects. Insects form the largest group of animals on earth.

Butterflies are found in many, many places. But do they live in cities? How often do you see them in your neighborhood? Or just flying down a city street? Like all animals, butterflies need food, water, shelter, and protection. But in most cities it is hard for them to find what they need.

In this chapter, we will learn how butterflies grow and live. Why do they need green spaces? How does the city affect butterflies? Read and find out.

96

THE BUTTERFLY LIFE CYCLE

The flying butterfly you see is
an adult insect. But before becoming
an adult, a butterfly must go through
metamorphosis. This means "to change
in shape." There are four stages in
a butterfly's life--the egg, the
caterpillar, the chrysalis, and the
adult. During each stage the butterfly
has a different shape and leads a
different kind of life. The butterfly's
shape shows its age.

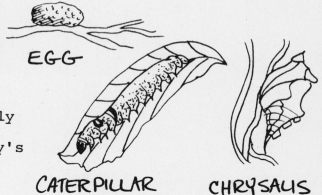

EGG

CATERPILLAR   CHRYSALIS

The Egg

Butterflies, like all other animals,
start from eggs. Butterfly eggs are not
laid in nests. Instead, they are attached
to the undersides of plant leaves. There
they are protected from hungry enemies,
from hot sun, and hard rains.

Many eggs are laid together, and
each one is very small. A magnifying
glass will help you find them. When you
do find them, look at the eggs closely.
Not all butterfly eggs are alike. This is
because there are many kinds of butterflies.
Some of them lay round eggs. Others lay
flat ones. How many other kinds of eggs
can you find?

The Caterpillar

Inside each egg is a living young
butterfly. In this shape the butterfly
is called the caterpillar. It has no
wings. In fact, it doesn't look like a
butterfly at all. It looks like a worm
with legs.

When it is ready, the caterpillar
hatches out of the egg. After hatching,
caterpillars do only one thing--eat,
and eat, and eat, and eat. The
caterpillar is the butterfly's growing
shape. Caterpillars eat so they can grow.

All caterpillars eat only the plants on which they are born. Plants are made largely of cellulose. These are tough fibers that support the plant. Since cellulose is very hard to digest, caterpillars must remove the food they <u>can</u> digest from the plant cellulose. Then they <u>must</u> discard the part they can't digest. To get enough nourishment from the plants, caterpillars must eat constantly.

Caterpillars can also be protected by the plants they eat. Some caterpillars look like part of a green leaf or a twig. This makes them hard to find.

The Chrysalis

When the caterpillar stops growing it spins a pad of silk. From this pad, it will hang upside down on its food plant. Soon its skin will break open and drop away. Hanging there instead will be an object that looks like a bag. This is the butterfly's resting shape, or <u>chrysalis</u>. The caterpillar in the chrysalis doesn't eat or move. But fantastic changes are taking place.

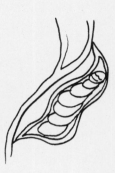

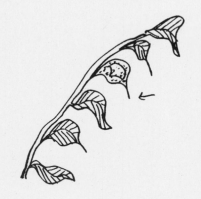

Inside the chrysalis, all the old caterpillar parts are being broken down. They are being rearranged to make the adult butterfly. While in the chrysalis, the butterfly is very helpless. It can easily be eaten by a hungry animal. Some chrysalises have defenses against their enemies, though. They take on the shape and color of the plants they are hanging on. Or they may resemble dried leaves or sharp thorns.

When it is ready, the chrysalis will break open. A new butterfly adult will emerge. Its wings will be wet and crumpled. But after a day or two, they will dry and spread out. Then the new adult butterfly will be ready to fly.

98

The Adult Butterfly

Most adult butterflies live by drinking nectar. Nectar is like sugar-water, and it is found in most flowers. Butterflies drink with a long, hollow tube that is coiled under their heads when they are not using it. This is the proboscis. When it is unrolled, it is like a drinking straw.

Adult butterflies cannot bite or sting. They fly slowly. Since they don't have much protection of their own, they depend on plants for protection. In sunny weather, the shade of plant leaves forms certain special patterns. The wings of some butterflies copy these shadow patterns in color and design. When these butterflies rest in the shadows, they seem to disappear. They are "invisible" until they fly again.

Other butterflies look like part of a plant. They have wings with the shape of living or dead leaves. These butterflies become very difficult to see.

Some butterflies have a very bitter taste. They signal their bad taste with bright colors, called warning colors. If a bird eats one of these butterflies, it will never do so again. The bright colors help the bird remember its bad-tasting lesson.

Many other butterflies do not have a bad taste. But they pretend they do. They copy the bright wing colors of the bad-tasting butterflies. The butterflies that do this are called mimics. You know about mimics. They pretend to be something they are not.

99

PLANTS HELP BUTTERFLIES . . .

When a butterfly becomes an adult, it
has completed its life cycle. The cycle
begins again when adult butterflies lay new
eggs and then die. Each part of the
butterfly's life cycle seems completely
different. Yet have you noticed that
there is one thing butterflies need during
every stage of life? They need green plants--
for food, for protection, and for places to
live.

Butterflies are dependent on plants
because, like other animals, they cannot
use the sun's energy directly to make food.
Plants, as we know, can use sunlight to
make the food they need to grow. But animals
must get their food indirectly, from plants
and other animals. So butterflies cannot
live without plants.

. . . AND BUTTERFLIES HELP PLANTS

Butterflies need plants. And flowering
plants, in turn, are important to many
butterflies. Plants reproduce themselves
with seeds, instead of eggs. The seeds are
made in their flowers. However, a special
powder is needed to start seed-making. It
is called <u>pollen</u>.

When adult butterflies visit certain
flowers to drink nectar, their bodies
become dusted with pollen. As they visit
other flowers, some of this pollen falls
off. The flowers that receive the pollen
can then start making seeds. This is
called <u>pollination</u>. The butterflies that
carry pollen are known as <u>pollinators</u>.

Next to bees, butterflies are our
best pollinators. Some flowers, such as
violets, would not be pollinated without
butterflies. We can see how butterflies
and plants need each other.

Butterflies and Adaptation

As we know, there are many kinds of butterflies and many kinds of plants. Imagine all butterflies feeding on the same kind of plant. If there were more plants than butterflies, there would be no problem. Each butterfly would get its share of food.

But what would happen if there were more butterflies than plants? Then the supply of butterfly food would not be large enough for all the butterflies. Each butterfly would try to get its share of food before another did. They would be in competition with each other. When there is too much competition, many butterflies will die.

Adaptation is the reason that competition has not killed off all butterflies. Adaptation means that butterflies have gone through certain changes. They have learned to eat different kinds of plants in order to survive. Most butterflies now use their own special plants, both for food and for shelter and protection.

All these adaptations did not happen at once. They came about bit by bit over many, many years. Nearly all natural changes are slow. In time, varieties of butterflies have become completely different from one another. And, because these different butterflies eat different kinds of plants, many butterflies can live together in the same place.

CAN BUTTERFLIES AND CITIES SURVIVE TOGETHER?

Cities are people-places. They are not made by nature. As cities grow, the land is cleared for buildings, factories, and streets. Almost overnight, green plants are replaced by concrete, glass, and steel.

Butterflies don't survive well under these conditions. They don't have enough time to adapt to the sudden changes that often take place in cities. Only certain spaces, such as parks and large gardens, are still suitable for butterflies' needs.

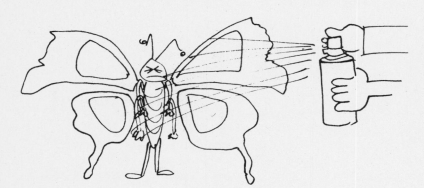

Often, too, butterflies are killed by <u>pesticides</u>. Pesticides are chemicals that are used to kill <u>pests</u> such as flies and mosquitoes. Sadly, they often kill good insects, too. So, although we want more butterflies and fewer flies, what happens in cities is often the other way around.

LEARN MORE BY YOURSELF--OBSERVE METAMORPHOSIS

Spring and summer are "butterfly seasons." In the city, search carefully in parks, vacant lots, and large gardens. You may see butterflies in egg, caterpillar, chrysalis, or adult shape. If you find a caterpillar, you can observe metamorphosis.

If you go to the country, you will probably see many, many butterflies. Observe as many of them as you can, but <u>be sure not to catch and kill them.</u> Since more and more buildings, roads, and parking lots are being built everywhere, there are fewer and fewer places where butterflies can thrive. Some of them are in danger of becoming extinct. So we do not want to kill any of them.

Bring a caterpillar and a
piece of its food plant home.

Equipment You Will Need

1 large cardboard box

A piece of cheesecloth

A large, wide-mouth glass jar

Cotton

Tape

Additional plants of the kind
on which the caterpillar was
found.

What to Do

Make an opening (like a window) in the box. Put the plant
on which you found the caterpillar in a jar of water. Plug the
top of the jar around the plant stem with cotton. Place the jar,
plant, and caterpillar in the box. Cover the hole with cheesecloth, held on with tape. Replace the food plants with fresh ones
as the plants begin to wilt or rot.

Observation

Observe the stages the butterfly goes through as it becomes
an adult. After the adult has emerged from the chrysalis, wait
a day or two for its wings to dry before you release it to fly
free outdoors.

CHAPTER FOURTEEN

Clean Up After Your Dog, Please!

"A dog is man's best friend." It is easy to see why this is a popular saying. Dogs are fun to play with. They're lovable and cuddly. They keep us company when we're lonely. They protect us. Dogs such as seeing-eye dogs, sheep dogs, and police dogs work hard for us.

But dogs can also cause problems for people. They might bark at night when we want to sleep. They might frighten or hurt us when they're left off the leash. They might run away from home and become wild. And they use our streets and sidewalks as their bathroom. That's the biggest problem of all.

Cities have more pollution problems than anywhere else. The air and water are dirtier. The streets are noisier. And there is more garbage to collect and get rid of. There is more litter on city streets. And dog litter is a bigger problem in the city than in the country, too.

Dog litter makes city streets and parks look and smell ugly. Children fall in it. Everyone walks in it. No one likes to look at it. But there it is--all around us. How will we get rid of it? Will our city streets become just one big toilet for dogs?

Not everyone agrees about the solution to this problem. Some people get so disgusted that they want to keep all dogs out of the city. Some people give up and say there is nothing we can do about the problem. And still other people think that dogs and people can live together in harmony if dog owners will be good neighbors and clean up after their dogs.

Read on and find out why we feel dog litter is a problem. Think about the solutions we discuss. Then see if you can come up with some solutions of your own.

DOG LITTER PROBLEMS

Dog Litter Is Unpleasant

Dog litter makes it unpleasant to walk on city streets. On a hot day, dog droppings smell. And do you really want to walk around with your head down all day so you can be sure you don't step in the wrong place? Did you ever have to stop and wipe your shoes because you didn't look where you were walking? Ugh!

It Harms Grass and Trees

There is a chemical in dog urine and droppings that harms grass and trees. Cities need all the healthy green plants they can get. Green plants in the city need protection from dogs.

It Can Make You Sick

Flies like to be around dog droppings, and flies can carry all kinds of diseases to people. Dogs affect your health in other ways too. They aren't allowed in food stores because they might get germs on the food. And there is a certain disease that young children can get from dog droppings. It is called <u>toxicariasis</u>.

It Doesn't Decompose on Concrete

When plants and animals die, they decompose and become part of the soil. This is called a "cycle of nature." Animal droppings decompose and become part of the soil, too. But this happens more easily in the country than in the city. Can you guess why?

Wherever you look in a city, you see cement--streets, buildings, sidewalks, parking lots. When you take a dog for a walk, it is usually on a street or concrete sidewalk. All the soil is covered up. So most dog droppings don't get a chance to decompose and become part of the soil. Instead, they just sit on the street and wait for some unsuspecting person to come along!

DOGS OR PEOPLE?

Are Parks for Dogs or for People?

Sometimes city people can leave buildings and cement
behind and enjoy flowers and trees. City parks are popular
places on a nice day. It's fun to play ball or sit on the
grass with friends. Sit on the grass, that is, if a dog
didn't get there first.

Dogs like to run and play in parks
just as much as people do. But too many
people let their dogs use our parks as
dog toilets. Then it is hard for us to
enjoy the parks.

In the country, there isn't such a
problem. There is more room for both
dogs and people. But crowded cities
don't usually have enough parkland.
Every inch of park space is important
to city people.

Is Dog Litter a Dog Problem or a People Problem?

Whose fault is dog litter? Maybe we're really talking
about a people problem instead of a dog problem. Dogs are
pets. They have owners. And pet owners are the ones that let
dogs dirty our cities. After all, dogs can't clean up after
themselves, can they?

Many dog owners are very
careful not to throw litter
on the street. They use a
litter basket. But they go
right ahead and let their
dogs litter our streets and
sidewalks. They keep their
houses clean, but they let
their dogs dirty our parks.
They work hard to make their
neighborhoods pretty, but let
their dogs kill flowers, grass,
and trees. They don't understand that their dogs are
harming our environment.

What can we all do about
this problem? Is there any
solution? What do other
people think?

106

SOLVING THE DOG LITTER PROBLEM

Curb Your Dog

Some communities tell dog owners to walk their dogs only on the street near the curb. This is called "curbing" a dog. Then, when the sanitation department cleans the streets, it cleans away the dog litter, too.

Curb and Clean Up After Your Dog

Will curbing dogs solve the dog litter problem? Many people say no. They think that dog owners should curb their dogs and clean up after them, too.

Even when dogs are curbed, some streets have so many dogs that dog litter problems are very serious. The sanitation department usually can't clean the streets every day. What happens on the days the streets aren't cleaned?

There is an organization in New York City called PICK-UP. PICK-UP believes that dog owners should be good neighbors and pick up all kinds of litter, including dog litter. (Dogs can't clean up after themselves, remember.) People who are members of PICK-UP are not <u>against</u> dogs, they are <u>for</u> people. They are for people who want to enjoy their parks. They are for people who don't like to step in dog droppings. Mostly, they are for people who love dogs but want to be good neighbors, too.

There are many groups like PICK-UP in all parts of the country. These groups have dog owners as members, and also people who don't own dogs. They believe that cleaning up after your dog is the best solution to dog pollution.

Many places have passed laws to make people curb and clean up after dogs. Nutley, New Jersey, was the first town in the country to do this. In Nutley, everyone must curb his dog first, and then clean up after the dog. If a person doesn't clean up, a policeman can give him a ticket and make him pay a fine.

HOW CAN YOU CLEAN UP AFTER YOUR DOG?

Is it hard to clean up after your dog? Is it messy? Actually, it is not hard or messy at all. New products have been invented that can make cleaning up after your dog really easy. You don't have to get close to the dog droppings or get your hands dirty. It does take a little extra time, though.

"Pooper-scoopers" come in all shapes and sizes. With a pooper-scooper, the dog owner picks up his dog's droppings and puts them in a sanitary bag or box. Then he throws the sealed droppings into a garbage can or basket. All clean and neat!

Will "Clean-Up-After-Your-Dog" Laws Work?

Laws work best when people care. That is why many organizations are working hard to educate dog owners about the problems of dog litter. They are sure that dog owners will cooperate if they understand how dog litter harms our environment.

Paper-Train Small Dogs

Dog trainers say that it is possible to train small dogs so that they don't have to go outside. They can learn to use newspaper on the floor instead. Then the owner can throw the droppings in the garbage.

MORE IDEAS

Some people feel that dogs should not be allowed in the city at all, or not allowed in some parts of the city. They want to let dogs live only in houses that have backyards, for example, not in apartment houses. In Paris, dogs are not allowed inside most parks.

Other people think that the city government should charge dog owners a high tax for their dogs. This way people would be discouraged from keeping dogs. There is a problem doing this, though. Only poor people would be prevented from having dogs. Rich people could easily afford to pay the tax and have as many dogs as they wanted. This isn't fair.

WHAT CAN YOU DO?

Set a Good Example

If you own a dog, don't pollute your neighborhood with dog litter. Curb your dog. Use a pooper-scooper. If you set a good example, other people will copy you.

Investigate

Are there dog litter problems in your neighborhood? Look in the parks. Take pictures. Check sandboxes where little children play. (Did you know some cities don't allow dogs in zoos and playgrounds?)

Talk to People

Tell people what you think about this problem. Explain the problem of dog litter to them. Write letters. Don't fight with people. It is hard to explain things to people when they're angry.

Check your local pet store. Do they sell pooper-scoopers? Ask the store to sell them. Then tell people where the store is.

Make a Pooper-Scooper

Make your own ecological pooper-scooper. Re-use an old plastic bag. Put it over your hand, pick up the droppings, and then pull the plastic bag inside it. Tie the bag and throw it away.

Get Together

Form a group. Work with scouts, school clubs, ecology clubs. Fight litter. All kinds.

LEARN MORE BY YOURSELF

1. Write for more information. You can't convince people that dog litter is a problem if you don't know what you're talking about. The Environmental Protection Administration in New York City has a free pamphlet called "Dog Owners Guide to Scooping." Write to: E.P.A., Office of Public Information, Municipal Building, New York, New York 10007.

2. Find out if your city has a "curb and clean up after your dog" law. Who supported it? Who was against it?

3. Find out the different ways sanitation departments clean the streets of litter and dog droppings. Is it necessary to use a mechanical sweeper and a manual broom? What is a flusher? What happens when cars are parked the day a street is supposed to be cleaned?

CHAPTER FIFTEEN

Roaches Are a Special City Problem

Did you know that city children often share their homes and schools with one of the oldest living creatures on earth? It is a special kind of insect. Relatives of the insect were on earth long before man. Look around your home and school. Do you see any?

Some are big and some are tiny. They are dark brown or light brown or black. They have thin, flat bodies and can slip into the tiniest spaces. They have six skinny legs and run very fast. In fact they run so fast, it is very hard to catch them.

These insects are hitchhikers. They travel around a lot. They are also burglars that hate the light and sneak around at night.

No city person has to be told what kind of insect we're talking about. It's a ROACH, of course.

ROACH ANCESTORS

Roaches have been on the earth for 300 million years. They crawled around even before there were dinosaurs. They lived in trees, wet mud, caves. When dinosaurs appeared, roaches walked around on top of them!

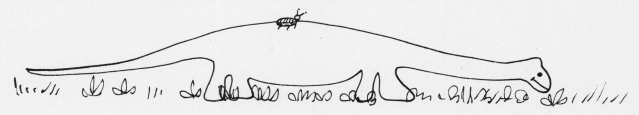

Scientists have found <u>fossils</u> of dead roaches in very old rocks. Do you know what fossils are? Fossils are the remains of plants or animals that lived in the past.

WHERE DO ROACHES LIVE?

In cities there are many buildings, and people living close together. Lots of people make lots of garbage. It is hard to keep the streets, parks, and buildings clean. Often landlords do not care enough about the buildings they own. They do not keep their buildings clean and repaired. There are always people, cars, buses, and trucks moving around in cities. These are some of the reasons why roaches like city living.

Roaches like to live in tiny places. They want to feel cozy and closed in. City buildings have many tiny cracks and hiding places where roaches can live. About 5 different kinds of roaches live in city buildings.

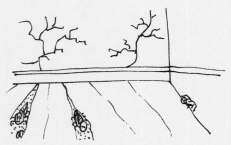

Roaches need a lot of water to drink. Some like to live in damp places. Big apartment houses have lots of water pipes. In old buildings, many water pipes leak. Roaches love leaking pipes.

Roaches also like dirty places! In cities there is usually garbage around for roaches to eat and hide in.

Once roaches get into a building they are hard to get out. If one apartment has roaches, other apartments may get them also. Roaches travel all through a building.

Roaches go from building to building, too. They ride in grocery bags, boxes, trucks. They can get into a brand-new, clean building this way.

HOW BAD ARE ROACHES?

Some insects are harmful. Some are helpful. Most insects live peacefully with people and are harmless. But roaches are a problem for people. They might be harmful. They bother people.

Roaches and Germs

Roaches can bring disease germs into your home and school. But they do not carry germs on their bodies. Roaches clean themselves. They lick their feet. So they swallow many germs. If they have eaten things that have germs on them some germs will die in their stomachs. Other germs are stronger and will stay alive.

Roaches leave little black droppings wherever they go. The strong germs that stay alive in roaches might be in these droppings.

Roaches and Your Health

Most droppings don't have germs in them. Scientists have never proven for sure that roach droppings harm people. But they know the germs are there. So there is a chance that you could get sick from touching or eating roach droppings. Someday scientists may know more about roaches and your health.

Roaches Stink!

There is an ugly odor in a place that has many, many roaches.

Roaches Are Destructive

They eat food. They eat fabrics and books. Roaches are called <u>omnivores</u>. That means they will eat almost anything.

Roaches Annoy People

Sometimes roaches seem to be everywhere. People do not like feeling that tiny insects are running all over their house. They do not like opening a cabinet or picking up a piece of paper and seeing a little insect scurry out.

Roaches can outsmart people. They know when they are in danger. Different parts of their bodies let them know right away. They run so fast it's hard to catch them. They sneak out at night and nibble on your cookies and bread crumbs.

HOW TO RUIN ROACHES

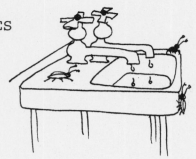

Take Away Their Water Supply

Keep the kitchen and bathroom dry.
Mop up spilled water. Have someone fix
leaky water pipes and dripping faucets.

Take Away Their Hiding Places

Don't give roaches places to hide.
Clean up piles of clutter. Pick up
things from the floor. Roaches don't
like neat rooms.

Go into a dark room. Turn on a
light. See where the roaches run to
hide. If they go to cracks in the walls,
fill up these cracks with plaster.

Keep Them Out of Your House

Check packages you bring home.
Is a roach hitchhiking in them?
Remember, roaches like to be in small,
snug places. Also, roaches come in
from other houses through cracks in
the walls and floor. Fill up these
cracks with plaster. Keep roaches
out.

Try to Starve Them

Roaches are not fussy eaters. They do not depend on one
kind of food. They will eat vegetables. They will eat meat.
They will even eat things like paint.

Roaches have been around for millions of years. The kinds
of plants and animals have changed in all that time. But roaches
have just learned to eat different foods. TV insulation and glue
are new foods for roaches. Roaches can even go without food for
a long time.

It's hard to starve a roach, but you should try. Don't
leave food around. Clean up crumbs from kitchen floors and
counters. Wrap or cover all food tightly.

HOW NOT TO RUIN ROACHES

Some people use poisons to try to kill roaches. These poisons are called <u>pesticides</u>. You can buy pesticides in cans at the store. Sometimes a person called an <u>exterminator</u> comes to spray special pesticides in your house.

Exterminators are busy people. They never really finish their job. There are always a few roaches that do not die from the exterminator's spray. They are too strong. They breathe the poisons, but they keep on living. These strong roaches get used to the pesticides. They have babies. Some of these babies are just as strong as their parents, or stronger. Pesticides do not kill them. So companies make stronger poisons. But there are always some stronger roaches that are not killed. This is one big reason why roaches are so hard to get rid of.

There is another problem with pesticides. They can hurt helpful insects at the same time they are hurting harmful ones. They can hurt you. Sometimes, pets die when strong pesticides are sprayed in the house.

Look at a pesticide can. The label says that it is dangerous. Be careful when the exterminator comes to your house. Ask the exterminator to be careful. Open the windows to let fresh air in.

The best thing to do is <u>not</u> to use pesticides at all. There are much safer ways to keep roaches out of your house. You might have to work a little harder, but you will help protect our environment.

ROACHES ARE ADAPTABLE

<u>Adaptable</u>. This means something can change easily. Roaches have lived millions of years because they are adaptable. Roaches continue to live even if their environment changes. As the earth changes, they just change their habits. There was a time when ice covered many parts of the earth. Many living things died. But roaches survived.

THINK OF ALL THE THINGS YOU HAVE LEARNED ABOUT ROACHES. WHY HAVE THEY SURVIVED?

Read

1. Cockroaches by Joanna Cole (William Morrow and Company, 1971). This is a whole book about roaches! It was written especially for young people. Find out more about a roach's body and habits. Learn how roaches can tell when you are going to hit them. Learn why roaches don't have many enemies.

2. Discovering Nature Indoors edited by Laurence Pringle (The Natural History Press, 1969). This book can help you learn about many kinds of small animals--all in your own home. You can study fish, ants, gerbils, flies, and ROACHES. Find out how to make a roach trap. Watch the roaches you catch. Try experiments. This book gives you lots of ideas for experiments. Learn about roach "schedules" and the kinds of homes they like best. Investigate the lives of roaches.

3. C.A.N., an organization in New York, has written a newsletter on pesticides for you and your parents. It explains why pesticides can be dangerous. Some pesticides are more dangerous than others. Read the C.A.N. newsletter with your parents. Learn about pesticides together. Write to: C.A.N., 49 East 53rd St., New York, N.Y. 10022. Ask for issue #5. Send 50 cents.

4. COCKROACHES: How to Control Them. This leaflet is put out by the Department of Agriculture. It describes the five kinds of cockroaches that live in city buildings. It gives hints on where roaches hide and how to get rid of them. It tells you how to be careful with pesticides. The leaflet recommends using some pesticides. Do you think this is a good idea? Try other ideas first. Send 10¢ to: Superintendent of Documents, U.S. Government Printing Office, Washington, D.C. 20402. Ask for leaflet #430.

CHAPTER SIXTEEN

Shhhhh! Too Much Noise!

In the past 100 years, the world has changed a lot. Many machines have been invented. These machines make other machines. People use small machines in their homes and at work. They use machines to go places and build things. There are thousands of kinds of machines. But what is one thing most of these machines have in common? They make noise.

Machines that make newspapers and books make noise. Cars, subways, and airplanes make noise. Even washing machines make noise. Some noises don't bother you. But some things make so much noise that they make it hard to talk or listen. And some noises can really be bad for you. This is one way the world has changed in the last 100 years. It's a noisier world today than when your grandparents were young. Today, we call the problem "noise pollution."

The world is full of different sounds. Not all sound is noise. Think of sounds that are not made by machines. Leaves rustle when the wind blows. Running water makes a splattery, sloshy sound. Birds make swooshing, whirring sounds when they fly. People make sounds when they talk, laugh, clap. Music is also a special type of sound.

Sound becomes noise when it is too loud--when it interferes with what we are saying or doing--when it hurts our ears--when it makes us nervous--or when it is just unpleasant to hear. In this chapter, we will tell you about what noise does to you and what you can do about noise.

HOW DO YOU HEAR?

To understand noise pollution, it's important to understand how the ear works. The "outer ear," the part you can see and touch, acts like a funnel. It catches all the sound and sends it to your "inner ear." The inner ear has a canal which leads to the eardrum. The eardrum acts very much like the drum in an orchestra. It has a very thin layer of skin that vibrates when sound waves hit it. The inner side of the eardrum then moves tiny bones inside your head. When these bones move, they vibrate tiny hairs that are connected to nerves. These nerves run to your brain. Your brain then receives the information that your ear is hearing sound. Your brain tells you how to react to that sound. If the sound is too loud, you may cover your ears with your hands so you won't hear it. If the sound is nice, you will stay with it. You like it.

Clatter, screech, crunch, boom, zap. Read more about noise and your ear. Look up books in the library under <u>ear</u>, or <u>sound</u> or <u>noise</u>. Ask your doctor to explain to you how the ear works. What does he see when he looks in your ear?

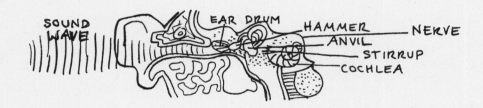

LISTEN!

Just close your eyes and listen for a long time. Try doing this in different places. Listen near your home. Listen outside and inside. Listen in a crowd and when you are alone. Listen on a street and in a park. Listen near a building that is being constructed. Listen to a rock group, to someone singing different songs, to TV, and the radio.

Some people love really loud sounds. They dig big noise. Most people don't. They would rather hear the quiet sounds of a park than a jet plane or a honking car. Concentrate very hard when you hear these sounds in different places. Try to figure out what you feel. Do you feel nervous? Like screaming? Do you feel like singing and smiling? Does your stomach hurt? Do your ears hurt? Does your heart beat faster? Do you feel happy and relaxed?

Listen for patterns in sounds. Some noises made by trains
and cars are ugly. But can you hear good sounds in the city, too?
Can you hear sounds that are like music?

Some people are hooked on noise. It's a habit. They always
have the TV or radio on. Do you think they're really listening?
Or are they just filling up the silence? That's hard to answer.
Try to be by yourself for a while. Just listen in the silence.

SHUT UP! THAT NOISE IS KILLING ME!

How many times have you heard that? Do parents or teachers
ever say that to you? Scientists have discovered that loud sounds
give people stomach aches and headaches, make their hearts beat
faster, make them tired and angry. Even sound that is not very
loud can disturb us. Can you think of a sound that is not too
loud, but that bothers us because it lasts a long time? Or a
sound that is not very loud, but that interrupts what we are
doing--like a telephone ringing?

Doctors and scientists know that too much sound hurts your
ears. It can even make you a little deaf. The more loud sounds
you hear, the more harm is done to your ears. After a sudden,
big noise, or after a long time of being exposed to loud noise,
your ears may start ringing. Has this ever happened to you?
Noise makes the eardrum vibrate. When it vibrates too fast for
too long, your ears start ringing.

Noises in a city make us nervous and edgy. They even make
us feel angry at people for no reason. Try standing and talking
to a friend near a construction site or a jackhammer for a long
time. How do your ears feel? Do you start to feel impatient?
Are you angry at the noise makers? Does the noise make you feel
old and tired?

MEASURING NOISE

Air and water pollution can be measured. So can noise pollution. Noise is measured by <u>decibels</u>. The very softest sound you can hear is one decibel--like one leaf blowing in the wind. A sound 10 times stronger is about like a strong wind blowing. A sound of 50 decibels is like a dishwasher. A garbage truck or subway car is about 100 decibels. A regular, healthy ear can get those ringing sounds or can be made deaf for a while by sounds of 100 decibels or more. Jet planes make sounds of 150 decibels if they fly over you. When someone shoots a gun, it makes a sound of about 140 decibels. A rock and roll band's sound is about 120 decibels.

FIND THE NOISE MAKERS IN YOUR HOME

Make a list of the machines in your home. Do you have a vacuum cleaner? A TV? A hair dryer? What other machines does your family have? What ones make noise? Is the noise pleasant or unpleasant?

Do you really need all these machines? Remember, using fewer machines makes things quieter. It saves electricity, too. And that saves your parents money on their electric bill. Remember also that a power plant makes the electrical energy your home uses. These power plants cause air pollution. So you are causing some air pollution when you use electricity in your home. You can't see it happening, but it is. Try to use fewer machines. It's quieter. It also helps keep the air a little cleaner.

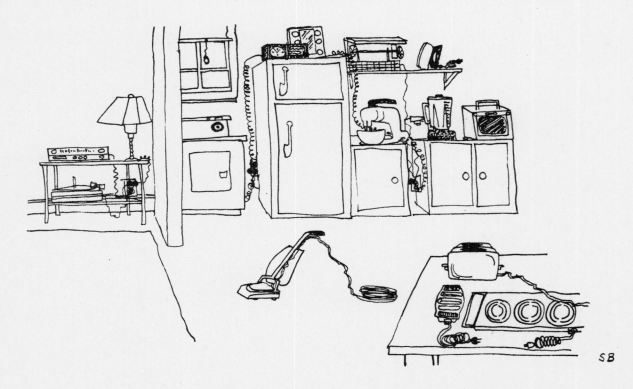

120

WHAT CAN YOU DO ABOUT NOISE?

In Your Home

Draperies and carpets help cut down noise. The thick cloth absorbs the sound so some of it doesn't reach your ears. Turn TV and radios down. Turn them off if you're not watching or listening.

Walk over to a person when you want to talk to him. Don't yell across the room. Yelling is noisy. It can also hurt your throat.

Think about

the other

guy

before

you

make

NOISE!!!

In Your School

Try not to shout inside the school building. If you feel like screaming, or being angry, shout when you are outside. Try to keep the teacher from shouting. Everyone will be more relaxed that way. Ask your principal to turn down the PA system, microphones, and bells if they are very loud. Noise makes people angry. When you're angry, you feel like making more noise. And this makes people even more angry.

<u>In Your Town or City</u>

Find out who the noise control people are in your city government. Ask them questions about noise. Are there any laws to keep people from making too much noise? Who can you call to report people who are breaking the noise laws?

YOU CAN LEARN MORE BY YOURSELF

<u>Read</u>

1. <u>The Listening Walk</u> by Paul Showers (Thomas Y. Crowell Company, 1961). This is a "Let's-Read-and-Find-Out-Science Book." It is for younger children. With this book you can take a walk and discover sounds. Try to make these different sounds yourself. Close your eyes. Figure out where the sounds come from.

2. <u>Our Noisy World</u> by J. G. Navarra (Doubleday and Company, Inc., 1969). This is for older children. It explains sources and causes of noise pollution.

<u>Write</u>

1. <u>Noise and You</u>. You can get this 25¢ booklet from Channing L. Bete Co., Inc., Greenfield, Mass. 01301. You can learn more about how your ear works and how sound is measured. It also tells you what noises are dangerous and how to protect your hearing.

2. Newsletter #4 about noise pollution is from a group called Consumer Action Now (C.A.N.). Send 50¢ to C.A.N., 49 East 53rd Street, New York, N.Y. 10022.

CHAPTER SEVENTEEN

Moving Around

Big cities are places full of movement. People walk and ride. Trucks rumble by, and load and unload. Fire engines and police cars speed from place to place. Even during the night, there is movement. Cities never seem to sleep.

Why is there so much movement in large cities? Is it because no one likes to relax or stand still? Or is all this moving around really necessary?

As you know, cities are big, crowded places. Millions of people live, work, and play in cities. And living, working, and playing can't be done without lots of movement.

Transportation moves people and things from one place to another. Most of us use some kind of transportation every day. Even walking is a form of transportation. Grown-ups travel to work by bus, train, car, or bicycle. Children walk, bike, or ride a bus to school. Trucks carry workers and equipment to many different jobs. Without all kinds of transportation, there would be no cities.

So, transportation is an important part of the city environment. It affects the way we live. And it affects the cities we live in. All of us need to understand how and why we use it.

People have always used transportation. Long ago, even before there were towns, people needed to go back and forth to their fields. They had to move around to find animals and wild plants to eat. They had to carry things from place to place.

Did early people use the same kinds of transportation we use today? Did they have trains and airplanes to take them on long journeys? Can you imagine cave dwellers driving cars?

Those long-ago people didn't have the fast transportation we are used to today. Most of them walked from one spot to another. They carried their burdens on their backs. A few lucky ones had animals to ride and to carry their belongings. Many people tried to live near rivers or oceans. They could then build boats for easier transportation.

The early ways of traveling were very slow. So almost all people were <u>isolated</u>. This means that they had to stay close to the places where they were born. It was hard to move far away. They knew almost nothing about other groups of people.

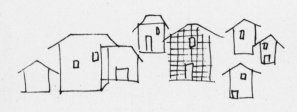

After a long, long time, some people got tired of being so isolated. Groups of them found spots where more people could live near each other. They felt safer where they had many neighbors. They could exchange things they grew and made. Gradually, these places became small cities.

. . . BUT VEHICLES WENT A LITTLE FASTER

Those first cities didn't look very much like the cities we know today. They were not very large. They were "walking cities." People moved around mostly on foot. They lived near their work. Sometimes they did their work in the same house where they lived.

Many people in cities wanted to trade with people in other cities. But carrying things between the small cities was very slow. So vehicles, such as wagons and carriages, were invented.

Soon vehicles were made to go faster. They could be pulled by one animal, or by more than one. For instance, a large carriage might be pulled by a team of four or six horses. With each horse that was added, the carriage increased its pulling power. It could then go faster. We still measure the power of transportation by horsepower. You may have heard your parents talk about how much horsepower the engine of your car has.

Boats were built to be bigger and faster, too. In the beginning, they were rowed or paddled by one or two persons. Bigger boats could be rowed or paddled by more people. Soon sails were invented to use the energy of the wind. When the wind pushed the sails, the boats went faster.

As city people used better vehicles they became less isolated. But their transportation was still much slower than ours today. For hundreds of years, people kept on using the same old ways of traveling. They walked and they rode animals. They used vehicles drawn by animals or pushed by water and wind.

About 250 years ago, an important invention made enormous changes in transportation! This invention was the steam engine. Transportation was never the same after the steam engine. And the big changes that it brought made big changes in the environment of cities.

The steam engine used a new kind of energy. It used the energy of burning coal to boil water and create steam. The steam's energy moved pieces of metal called pistons. The moving pistons were attached to wheels. The force of the moving pistons moved the wheels. Smoke from the burning coal went out a smokestack.

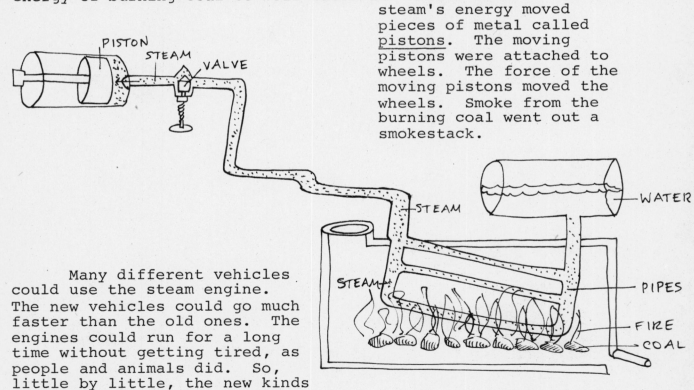

Many different vehicles could use the steam engine. The new vehicles could go much faster than the old ones. The engines could run for a long time without getting tired, as people and animals did. So, little by little, the new kinds of transportation replaced the old ones. There was fast, safe, and easy travel between cities at last.

. . . AND THE ENGINES PULLED LOTS OF WHEELS

The first important vehicle to use the steam engine was the railroad train. Railroads were built between one old city and another. New cities grew up by the railroads that spread through the countryside. These new railroad cities did not have to be near rivers or oceans to have good transportation.

Railroad cities grew quickly. They looked more like the cities we see today. They were the first modern cities. Railroads ran out of their centers like the spokes of a wheel. Many factories were constructed along the train lines in the cities. These were soon called the "factory belts." City workers built new homes near the factories so they could be near their work.

Other workers moved outside the "factory belts" into the countryside. They used the railways to get back and forth to the cities. Soon the cities began to spread out all around. They got larger and larger. They were no longer the old "walking cities."

The railways had solved the problem of fast transportation between one city and another. But there were now problems getting from place to place inside the larger cities. More and more workers lived too far from their jobs to walk to work.

City people did not want to use steam engines inside their cities. Steam engines burned coal. Coal smoke was black, smelly, and sooty. It made the cities dirty and unhealthy. So inventors tried to find new kinds of fast transportation to use inside cities.

ELECTRIC TRAINS ARE FAST AND CLEAN . . .

The use of <u>electricity</u> changed travel inside cities. Scientists had known a little about electricity for hundreds of years. But in the 19th century, they invented ways for people to use electricity.

Electricity made it possible to run engines without steam. Electrical energy was produced by a <u>generating plant</u>. It was carried to train engines by wires. Electrical energy gave the power to turn the wheels of vehicles. And electric engines didn't give off dirty smoke. Soon many of the horse-drawn trolleys were replaced by electric trolleys. And passenger railroads were built to run by electricity inside the cities.

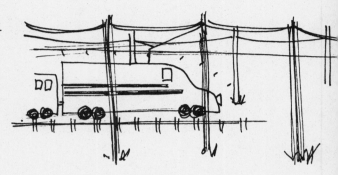

These electric trolleys and railways were able to travel swiftly. But cities were becoming large and crowded. It was sometimes impossible for the electric vehicles to move quickly through all the street traffic.

About 80 years ago cities started to build a new kind of electric railway--underground. The first one in our country was in Boston. Soon afterwards New York City constructed the first miles of its "subway." It is still the largest underground railway in the world.

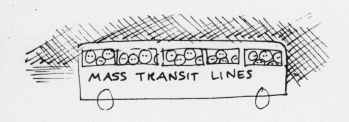

Trains on the new underground railways could go very fast. They did not have to stop for other traffic. And they could carry thousands of passengers each hour. These railways are still in use today. They are the first examples of good <u>mass</u> <u>transportation</u>.

. . . BUT WE STILL LOVE THE AUTOMOBILE

You would feel right at home in the cities of the early 20th century. In many ways they looked much as cities do today. There were lots of walkers. Trolleys criss-crossed the streets and avenues. Electric trains rumbled underground.

But you would notice one important difference--long ago there were no automobiles! Like the steam engine and the electric train, the invention of the car changed transportation in big, important ways. The automobile has changed city transportation more than any other vehicle.

The modern automobile does not run on steam or electricity. It has a combustion engine. The energy of burning gasoline fumes forces the pistons to move. The pistons move the wheels. The smoke from the burning gasoline goes out the back of the car through the exhaust pipe.

The invention of the automobile gave people quick transportation. It gave "door-to-door" service. People didn't have to walk from place to place. They didn't even have to walk to the nearest stop of the trolley or underground railway. They could swap their horses and buggies for "horseless carriages."

Everyone wanted cars. But there are more cars now than we ever dreamed of. In some ways the automobile has improved transportation. But it has also caused problems for cities. Now many people are wondering if the automobile is such a blessing.

How different cities are today from the days of the "walking cities!" Today's transportation is a big part of the city environment. Often, it makes our lives easier. But the ways we travel can also make our air dirty. Transportation can be a cause of noise pollution, too. And our ways of traveling have a big effect on the way we use land.

A city with a good environment has a good <u>quality</u> <u>of</u> <u>life</u>. A good quality of life in a city means that people can live happy and healthy lives there. They can enjoy the city without a lot of environmental pollution.

Since transportation affects our environment, it also affects the quality of life. Transportation does more than just move people or things from one place to another. It also helps to make cities pleasant or unpleasant places to live in.

MOVING AROUND USES UP LAND . . .

Natural resources are a part of
our environment. Resources are many
things, including air, water, and
land. Land is one of a city's most
important natural resources. There
are many ways that people want to
use it.

In the long-ago days of "walking
cities," slow transportation made it
hard to use land that wasn't nearby.
Land in the cities was easy to get to.
Everyone wanted to use that land, so
it became very valuable. It had to
be used wisely.

But, in modern times, city
land has often not been used
carefully. City lots are abandoned.
Enormous shopping centers waste
hundreds of acres. Many houses and
stores are built close together
without leaving room for open
green space. Expressways and
parking lots often destroy beautiful
neighborhoods.

Transportation by railway and automobile helped to
change the ways cities use land. It allowed people to move
out of the city centers. Cities spread beyond their old
boundaries, and roads were
built all over the place.
With cars for transportation,
people could live far away
from their work. There was
much more land that was easy
to get to. So land no
longer seemed so precious.

City people began to
get careless in the ways
they used land. Cities
spread and spread. Growth was not planned. It "just happened."
We even have a special name for this kind of waste. We call
it urban sprawl.

How does urban sprawl affect the quality
of life in cities? Does urban sprawl make
cities pleasant or unpleasant? To answer
these questions, we must understand the social
costs of transportation and urban sprawl.

Most of us think of costs as the amount of money we pay
when we buy something. But social costs are not always paid
with money. Sometimes they are paid with bad health or unhappy
lives. Social costs are often paid by everybody, whether they
want to pay them or not.

What are some of the social
costs of spread-out cities? As
cities grow, people use cars more
and more. There are fewer riders
for the trains and buses. In some
cities, the trains and buses may
be neglected. They may become
very old and dirty, or break down a lot. Sometimes public
transportation ceases to exist at all! Then people who can't
own or drive cars can't travel far away from home. This is
one social cost.

More and more these days, it is impossible
to get to some places without a car. People
who don't have cars are cut off from many nice
things that they would enjoy. Children and old
people miss out on things most of all. This is
another social cost.

When most people use cars for moving
around, many more roads are built. More
land is paved over with asphalt and
concrete for parking lots. Gas stations
and repair garages take up more space.
In some American cities, over half of
the land is turned over to the car!
There is less land that can be used for
the other things we want and need. This
is a terrible social cost.

132

THERE'S DIRTY AIR AND LOTS OF NOISE . . .

Other social costs of modern transportation are air and noise pollution. Most transportation causes some air pollution because of the fuels burned for its energy. The automobile causes the worst air pollution. The gasoline used in cars is not completely burned in the engines. So polluting fumes escape into the air.

Scientists have proved that the poisonous fumes from automobiles are harmful to people and plants. Sometimes, the fumes will combine with sunlight to form <u>photochemical</u> <u>smog</u>. Smog can cause us to cough. It can make our eyes water and hurt. Many doctors believe that air pollution from cars causes lung diseases.

Modern transportation also adds to noise pollution. Too much loud noise can be harmful to us. After hearing loud noises for many years, we can lose part of our hearing. Too much noise also makes us nervous and "jumpy."

Jet airplanes with loud engines are noise polluters. People who live near jetports have to put up with almost constant noise. Those in houses near expressways complain about the noise from cars and trucks. Train riders suffer when train wheels screech on steel tracks.

Sometimes it takes years to understand the effects of air and noise pollution on our health. Problems don't always show up right away. But they are a large part of the social costs we all have to pay.

How can we solve some of the problems we've created? Some experts think we can improve the transportation we have now. We can make cars that are smaller and weigh less. Smaller cars don't need such large roadways, parking lots, and garages. Their engines run on less fuel. And the engines can be designed to burn the fuel more completely. These new engines will put less poisonous fumes into the air.

Many city experts think we should use more mass transportation. Trains and buses don't pollute the air as much as cars do. They use less fuel to carry more people. Most big cities are suggesting that people leave cars at home and take trains or buses. Some cities are even refusing to build more super-highways. They want to use their money for mass transportation instead.

Other experts call for new ways to move around. They want high speed trains that run by the energy of magnets or air pressure. They have also suggested moving belts called "people movers" that could transport people easily around shopping centers. And they recommend that people use small electric cars in cities instead of big, polluting cars.

But don't forget the oldest ways of moving around! Many people still walk from place to place. Or they ride non-polluting bicycles. Transportation that doesn't pollute will improve the quality of life in cities. And there will be fewer social costs for all of us to pay.

What about your own life? How do you use transporatation? Are you a "polluter" or a "non-polluter"? Does urban sprawl affect you? The activities on the next two pages will help you think about the ways you move around.

1. A Transportation Math Problem

One railroad track can carry 72,000 people in one hour. One underground railway track can carry 60,000 people in one hour. A 3-lane highway can carry 6,000 people in one hour, if each car has 6 passengers.

a. Which kind of transportation carries the largest number of people?

b. Which kind of transportation carries the smallest number of people?

c. How many more people per hour can the railroad track carry than the 3-lane highway?

2. Urban Sprawl Checklist

Find out how urban sprawl affects you. Answer "yes" or "no" to each question below.

a. Does your family own a car?
b. Does your family have to own a car?
c. Must your parents drive you to the places you want to go?
d. Do most of your friends' families own cars?
e. Do many of them own more than one car?
f. Is it difficult for your family to use public mass transportation?
g. Do your parents need a car to go to work?
h. Do you need a ride to school?
i. Do you need a ride to the movies?
j. Do your father and mother need a car to go shopping?

Add up your answers. If you get more "noes" than "yesses," urban sprawl hasn't got you yet! Can you think of ways to change your "yesses" to "noes?"

TEST THE WAYS YOU MOVE AROUND

1.   <u>Plan a Trip</u>

     Choose an interesting spot for your destination. It might
be a museum, a park, an aquarium, or a zoo. Ask your parents or
teacher to get you a city transportation map. Decide the best
way to get where you want to go.

Is there . . .

a.   a train (either above ground
     or under the ground)?
b.   a city bus?
c.   a school bus?
d.   a private car?
e.   any other way?

     After you have made the plans, answer the following
questions:

a.   Which way takes the longest time?
b.   Which way takes the shortest time?
c.   Which way pollutes the least?
d.   Which way pollutes the most?

2.   <u>Make a Transportation Graph</u>

     Gather information from everyone in your class. Ask how
each travels to school. Some may walk, take a bike, train,
bus, or private car. Add the number of students in each
category. Put your information into a line graph or bar graph.
Your teacher can help you decide which kind to make.

a.   Which kind of travel is used by the
     largest number of students?
b.   Which kind of travel is used by
     smallest number of students?
c.   Do you think yours is a non-polluting
     class?

CHAPTER EIGHTEEN

Biking Can Be Beautiful

We all know that biking is a lot of fun. It gets us where we want to go. It provides good healthy exercise. But let's give some thought to biking and the environment. Do bikes cause air pollution the way cars, buses, and trucks do? These gasoline-powered vehicles put harmful pollutants into the air. But bikes don't get their power from gasoline. They need only "pedal power." And pedal power comes from the bike rider's own body energy.

All day long in our city streets we hear the honking of horns and the roaring of motors. But what kind of sound does a bike make? Does the swishing of pedals hurt our ears? Bikes don't cause air pollution. And they don't cause noise pollution either.

You've seen automobile junkyards and abandoned cars. But do you often see bicycle junkyards or abandoned bicycles dirtying up our streets and vacant lots? Do parked bicycles keep the streets from being properly cleaned? Of course not. And what about all the land that is covered up by roads, gas stations, and parking lots for cars? Did you know that fourteen bicycles can fit into the same space as one parked car? We could have a lot more parks and fewer parking lots if more people rode bikes instead of cars.

Less air pollution. Less noise pollution. Less land
pollution. Bicycling can help solve many of the problems of
our city environment. More and more people are beginning to
realize this. They are forming organizations all over the U.S.
to encourage biking for a cleaner environment. They even have
a special word for the idea. It is "bikeology." The word
"bikeology" puts bikes and ecology together. It shows how they
are related. In this chapter there are some ideas on how you can
be a part of the bikeology movement.

HELP FIGHT AIR POLLUTION--RIDE A BIKE

Motor vehicles--cars, buses,
and trucks--cause more air pollution than anything else in the
city. Many people say the car is
"anti-city." They want to dis-
courage private cars from being
used in the city because cars
make life in the city very
difficult for everyone. In what
ways? How would fewer cars in the
city help fight air pollution?
Would people want to keep buses
and trucks out of the city, too?

Bike riders care about air. They know that the air would
be cleaner if more people rode bikes instead of cars. Many
bicycle groups are having "bike-ins." They ride many miles in
parades to get attention! They want to remind people that bikes
are a clean form of transportation. In California a group of
young people in a bike club even took a pledge. They promised
to walk or use bikes to get to school and to visit each other.
They would ask their parents to drive them only during bad
weather or in a special emergency.

You can help fight air pollution, too. Try some of our
bikeology projects and think up projects of your own.

BIKE PROJECTS YOU CAN DO

1. Have a bike parade. Make posters that show how cars pollute the air and bicycles don't. Carry these posters in the parade.

2. Learn about the carbon monoxide and lead that cars put into the air. Tell other people about these harmful pollutants.

3. Keep a record of how often you ride in a car. How many of these trips were short trips? Could you have used your bike instead of asking your mom or dad to drive you?

4. Keep in shape by riding a bike. When you ride a bike you can burn up 100-120 calories every mile. Burning up calories by exercise is one way to lose weight. Take a bike ride. Figure out how many miles you rode. Multiply by 120. See how many calories you burned up. Find out how many calories a person has to burn up to lose a pound. Then figure out how many miles you have to ride to lose a pound.

5. Get your parents interested in bicycle riding. It is good for circulating the blood. It will keep them slender and healthy. And it's fun for families to bike together.

JOIN A BIKE CLUB

People who enjoy biking often join bike clubs. They meet new friends who like to bike. They go on bike trips together. Club members learn about biking from each other. They get to know the best places to go on trips. They find out which bikes are best for long trips. They learn how to fix their bikes themselves. Some bike clubs have a bike "cooperative." They collect used and broken bikes and recycle the bike parts. Do you think you could build a bike from old bicycle parts?

Some bike groups have symbols that show how they feel about biking and the environment. Two club symbols are on this page. Start your own bike club. Let people know how they can help the environment by biking. Design a symbol yourself. Or hold a contest in your school.

LEARN MORE BY YOURSELF

Read

Bike-ways (101 Things to Do with a Bike) by Lillian
and Godfrey Frankel (Sterling Publishing Co., Inc.,
1971). Young people can learn a lot about biking
from this book. It gives many ideas for bike clubs
and tells all about bike trips and bike camping.
You can also learn about different kinds of bikes
and how to take care of them. Do you know what a
bike rodeo is? Read this book and find out!

The Complete Book of Bicycling by Eugene A. Sloane
(Trident Press, 1970). This is a very good book
for your older brothers and sisters and parents.
It tells all about how to buy and care for a bike.
There is also information about bike trips and
camping and a short history of bicycling.
Remember, you want to get your parents interested
in biking. This would make a good present for them.

A Great Bicycle Book by Jane Sarnoff and Reynold
Ruffins (Charles Scribner's Sons, 1973. New
edition 1976). A fun book about bicycles that
includes not only information about the maintenance
and repair, but also riding and racing suggestions
and silly and serious facts about bicyles and
bicycle riding. Lots of safety suggestions, too.

Write

Bicycle Manufacturers Association of America, 1101
Fifteenth St., Washington, D.C. 20005. They have
many materials that would be of interest to you.
Ask them to send you the list. One booklet tells
you how to organize and enjoy bicycle clubs. One is
all about bikeways. They also have bike safety
posters and a bicycle safety set.

140

BIKEWAYS

Bikeways are roads, paths, and trails especially for bike riders. Sometimes bikeways are side streets that have only a small amount of automobile traffic. A bikeway can also be one lane of a street that is marked off for use by bike riders. Some streets become "instant bikeways" when they are closed to regular traffic on certain days of the week. A bikeway is often marked with signs so people can follow the path without getting lost. The signs also remind automobile drivers that there are bike riders in the area so they will be on the alert.

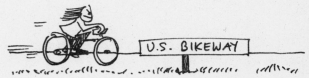

The first bikeway marked with signs in the U.S. opened in Homestead, Florida, in 1962. Today there are hundreds of bikeways all across the U.S. Some bikeways are only a few miles long and others are hundreds of miles long. Many bike groups want to have some of the bikeways joined together so that people can go all the way across the U.S. safely on a bike.

Bicycle groups are working hard to get more bicycle routes. But the job is not easy. First they have to figure out the best places for bikeways to be. Then they must get permission from the local transportation officials who are in charge of the roads and trails. Maps have to be drawn, too. Good maps are very important for good trips.

Is there a bikeway where you live? Find out. Call bicycle clubs and the Department of Transportation in your city. If there aren't any bikeways perhaps you can interest people in starting one.

BICYCLE PARKING

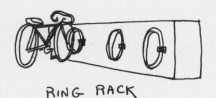

RING RACK

What would happen if tomorrow people in cities all over the U.S. started riding their bikes to stores and offices and schools? Where would they put their bikes when the got to their destination? In the street? Next to the desk in their offices? Think about it for a minute. There would be bikes stacked up and tangled up all over the place.

In Denmark, people ride bikes everywhere. Big cities like Copenhagen, Denmark, have bike racks for parking in front of stores and office buildings. But in the U.S. the movement to ride bikes in the city is just beginning, and there is a real bike parking problem.

SLOT RACK

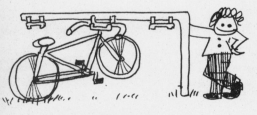

HOOK RACK

Many groups are trying to solve this problem so people will be encouraged to ride bikes. Biking organizations want garages to park bicycles as well as cars. Some commuters have formed associations to have space for bike parking set aside at train stations. In San Francisco people can now ride their bikes to many train stations and park them there. Some types of bicycle parking racks are shown on this page.

1. Find out how many cars a local garage can hold. Remember that 14 bikes can be parked in the space it takes to park one car. How many bikes could be parked in that same garage? Would we need fewer garages and parking lots if more people rode bikes instead of cars?

2. Take a survey of your neighborhood and your city. How many safe places are there for you to park your bike?

3. Design a bicycle parking rack. If you have a good design, send it to the Department of Transportation in your city, and to the Bicycle Manufacturing Association in Washington, D.C.

4. Does your school have bicycle racks? Are there enough spaces? Ask the principal of the school for more bicycle racks if you need them.

5. Do your teachers ride to work on bicycles? Get them to help you work for more parking spaces.

6. Get books out of the library about Denmark. Look at the pictures of people riding bicycles in Copenhagen and other cities. They will give you some good ideas for biking in your city.

CHAPTER NINETEEN

Places to Play

Everyone needs certain things to live. We need air to breathe and water to drink. We need food to eat and a place to live. We also need an environment that will help us have fun. Fun is very important to a person's spirit.

When people plan cities, they often forget to plan for play. There are special places for stores and office buildings. There are garages for cars and hospitals for sick people. But where are the places for people to relax and have fun?

Kids need places to climb, jump, slide, and yell. They need places to meet friends, play games, explore, and experiment.

In the country, this is easy. But not in our crowded cities. Land is disappearing in the cities. There aren't many green plants or trees. The streets are full of traffic.

A lot of city playgrounds aren't much fun either. They're often pretty boring. They're full of concrete. Lots of times they're locked up just when we want to use them!

Some people are trying to change this situation. They want to make our cities safe and fun to play in. They want to create "play environments" for boys and girls like you.

ADVENTURE PLAYGROUNDS

Adventure playgrounds are places where you can have adventures! You can explore, experiment, build, tear down, and build again. An adventure playground is what <u>you</u> want it to be.

The First One

Professor Sorenson was an architect who built beautiful playgrounds. One day he watched some kids playing in a vacant lot. He also saw some kids playing in a junkyard. Then he saw other kids playing in a construction site. These places were dangerous. They were messy. They certainly weren't beautiful. But the boys and girls were having more fun than in his beautiful playgrounds!

So Professor Sorenson decided to invent a new kind of playground. It would be a place where kids could do many of the things they did in vacant lots. They would be able to build things and experiment with materials. But there would also be a leader at the playground. A leader is an adult who can teach kids how to build things safely. He can give advice.

All this happened twenty years ago in Copenhagen, Denmark. The first adventure playground was very successful. The leader helped boys and girls have lots of fun. Today there are many adventure playgrounds in Europe. People are starting to build them in the United States also.

What Can You Do There?

Some people call adventure
playgrounds "do-it-yourself
playgrounds." That's because
kids build most things themselves.
The leader is there to give
advice, of course. He sees to
it that no one gets hurt.

Think of all the things you
could do with old tires, for
example. Make tunnels. Swings.
Obstacle courses. And what about
old lumber? One week you could
build a tower. Then rip it down
and build a slide or a workbench.

Some adventure playgrounds
teach arts and crafts. Many have
indoor areas for rainy days.
Others have outdoor stages for
plays. Whatever you want. In an
adventure playground, you just
use your imagination. Have an
adventure!

What Do They Look Like?

Adventure playgrounds are often
called "junk playgrounds." That's
because they're full of scrap
materials like old tires, lumber, and
bricks. These things aren't worth
anything to most people. But kids
who go to adventure playgrounds think
they are treasures. Of course,
adventure playgrounds are not very
pretty. So they often have fences
or bushes around them so people
outside won't see.

Adventure playgrounds never look
the same twice. They are always
changing. Kids are always building
something new. But there is one way
that adventure playgrounds never
look. They never look boring.
They never look like the concrete
playgrounds that cities often have.

MORE IDEAS FOR PLAY

People are trying to come up with other playground ideas. They want to design new kinds of play areas. They want to make the city more fun for kids. They want to bring a little of the country to the city. Some of their ideas sound pretty good to us. What do you think?

Apartment Building Play Space

Cities can sometimes be lonely places for kids. For little kids, especially. When playgrounds are too far away, their mothers won't let them go out alone. It is too dangerous for them to cross streets by themselves.

Planners of new apartment buildings have begun to think more about play spaces for little kids. Some are building parks and playgrounds right on the property of the apartment buildings. Kids don't even have to cross the street to have fun in a playground.

Small Parks

"Vest-pocket parks" are little parks near big city buildings. Sometimes they are built in lots where buildings have been torn down. Older kids can meet their friends here. Young children can come with their mothers. Adults can relax on benches and visit with each other.

Sometimes these parks are very expensive to build. Other times neighbors volunteer equipment and time. They build benches and plant flowers on streets themselves. The parks look very pretty and restful next to the tall concrete buildings. Why do you think they are called vest-pocket parks?

Water Fun

Kids love to play with water, especially in the summer time. Pools, puddles, sprinklers, hydrants, and fountains are all a lot of fun.

Some cities are looking for more ways to put water in parks and playgrounds. Many cities provide special caps for fire hydrants. These caps let kids play with the water right out in the streets without using it all up.

Sand and Dirt

Little children can spend hours sitting in a sandbox. They love to dig up dirt, make tunnels and mudpies.

Adventure playgrounds allow kids to dig up dirt. Sandboxes are a fun part of some playgrounds. But there are problems, too. Dogs can get into some sandboxes and leave their droppings there. This is not healthy for kids. Sand has to be raked daily too, to get rid of dangerous things like glass.

Animal Fun

How many animals do city kids get to see? Except for a few trips to the zoo they don't see many. And city kids hardly ever get to touch animals except cats and dogs.

One elementary school in New Haven, Connecticut, is doing something about this. The school keeps small farm animals outdoors in the spring. The kids can watch the animals and play with them. They can care for the animals, too. Do you think there should be animals in parks and playgrounds?

PLAYGROUND PROJECTS

Take a Survey

How many fun places to play are there where you live? Ask the kids in your school about their favorite play spaces. Do they like the school playground? Do many kids play in the street? Is it safe? Think of a lot of questions. Let everyone know the results.

Plan a Playground

If you could design a "play environment," what would it be like?

Fourth and fifth graders in Scarsdale, New York, formed a Playground Design Club. They met every week for a year with their art and math teachers. They did a lot of research. Each student made up his own designs.

The things they first wanted to do were too expensive. So they all designed one piece of equipment together. They called it their "Space Platform." Parents gave them money to have it built. It looks something like our drawing. One fifth grader said, "The children really love it . . . that's the best part."

There are many things to remember when planning a playground. Here are just a few of them. What other points can you think of?

1. Where will it be located?

2. Is it easy and safe to get to?

3. Will people who live nearby be bothered by the noise?

4. Who will use it?

5. What kind of equipment will be in it?

6. Is there protection from rain?

7. Is it sunny? Shaded?

8. Are there bathrooms nearby?

9. How much will it cost?

10. Who will take care of it?

Of course, designing a whole playground is a pretty big job. But you could start small. Design one piece of equipment. Use scrap materials, like tires.

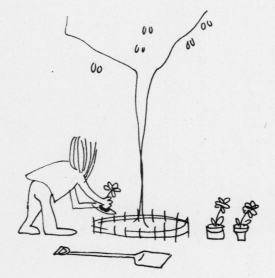

Fix Up a Playground

You can make playground areas nicer without spending much money. Fourth graders from a school in New York City are doing this. They cleaned up part of a nearby play area. They are going to plant flowers this spring. You could do this too. Or paint benches. Or scrub graffiti off walls. Or start a volunteer clean-up patrol. It's nice to have new play spaces, but it's important to take care of the old spaces, too.

CHAPTER TWENTY

An Apple a Day

Apples are beautiful. They taste delicious. They can be used in so many ways. And they're good for you.

You've heard the expression "An apple a day keeps the doctor away." That's because apples contain many important vitamins. We could also say "an apple a day keeps the dentist away." Apples have been called "nature's toothbrush" because they clean your teeth and gums.

Not all apples are alike. There are more than 700 varieties of apples in the world. They are different colors and sizes. Some are good for snacks. Others are good for cooking or baking.

Apples and apple trees are a part of our environment. How apples are grown, sold, and used affects our environment. That is what this chapter is all about. Read on. Try some of our apple activities. And eat an apple today.

NATURE'S PACKAGING

Visit a supermarket. Look around the fruit and vegetable department. How are apples wrapped for customers? Are they in little plastic or cardboard boxes? Are they wrapped in tissue paper? Are they in plastic or paper bags? Are little bags put in a big bag at the checkout counter? How much waste will be left over after these apples get home?

Is all this packaging necessary? Nature's packaging can be very good all by itself. Apple skins protect the apple from damage and germs, just as our skins protect us. Nature protects other fruits and vegetables too. Oranges, carrots, and potatoes all have skins that protect them.

Read the chapter on packaging in this book. Remember that people are throwing away more solid waste every year. It causes many problems in cities today. And too much packaging is a big part of the problem. Unnecessary packaging wastes natural resources. It pollutes the air when it is burned. It uses up valuable land when it is buried.

Find an old-fashioned fruit and vegetable stand. Or look at pictures of the way fruits and vegetables were packaged years ago. They used less packaging then. There was much less waste.

LEARN MORE BY YOURSELF

1. Take a survey of food stores in your neighborhood. Which stores package their apples the most? Which stores use the least packaging? Compare prices. Compare quality.

2. Investigate "nature's packaging." Peel a piece of skin from an apple. Gently scrape off any apple still stuck to the skin. Look at the skin under a microscope at school. What shape are the cells? Do you see spots of color in the cells?

MAKE AN APPLE POMANDER

Pomander balls keep closets, drawers, and rooms smelling nice and fresh. Sometimes they are mixtures of herbs and spices in a china or metal ball. But pomander balls can also be made with apples, oranges, lemons, or limes.

Make an apple pomander ball. Choose your apple carefully for this project. It must be small, red, and firm. Don't use an apple with any bruises on it. Use materials you have around the house for the packaging.

What You Will Need

1 firm, red apple	Ice pick or knitting needle
Whole cloves	A special covering for the apple
String and cotton cloth	(see #6 below)
Powdered cinnamon	A package for your pomander
1 ribbon 2 feet long	(see #7 below)

What to Do

1. Poke holes all over the apple with the ice pick or knitting needle. Be careful. Don't make the holes too close together. The skin will crack.

2. Push one clove into each hole.

3. Put the apple on a clean cotton cloth. Sprinkle with powdered cinnamon.

4. Tie the cloth around the apple. Hang it up to dry for 3 weeks.

5. Untie the cloth. Shake off the excess cinnamon.

6. Rewrap the apple in something that will let the nice odor escape, like cheesecloth, or part of an old nylon stocking. Attach ribbon for hanging pomander in closet.

7. If you are giving the pomander as a gift, design a package. Paint an old box. Make wrapping paper from magazine pages or comic strips.

APPLES--THE ORGANIC WAY

Apples are sometimes grown "organically." Many people believe organic apples are healthier for you. Organic gardening and farming is a special way of growing plants. Pesticides are not used. Artificial fertilizers are not used. Fruits and vegetables grown this way have no artificial chemicals added.

It's true that plants do need protection from harmful insects and plant diseases. They do need good soil to grow in. But organic farmers use nature to help the plants along instead of using chemicals. They use special rich soil. They let helpful birds and insects eat the harmful insects.

 Organic farming isn't simple. Sometimes it seems easier to just spray a lot of chemicals. But often the chemicals are hard to wash off the foods. They might make you sick. And pesticides can kill helpful birds and insects as well as pests. When it rains, chemicals can wash into rivers and harm fish, too. Organic farmers believe it is better to work with nature than against it.

From special companies, organic apple growers can buy thousands of helpful insects for their orchards. The farmers sometimes put nets over their small apple trees. Then harmful insects can't leave eggs on the trees. Organic farmers might also use a sticky paper to trap harmful crawling insects going up the trunk.

Why are we talking about organic farming in a book that's mostly for city kids? Well . . . city kids eat apples too, don't they? And these apples might have chemicals on them. We have learned about birds that migrate. The robin in your park might be poisoned by chemicals sprayed on trees 100 miles away. Rivers travel a long way. Chemicals washed into rivers upstream can be carried right past your city.

This is the lesson ecology teaches us. Everything in our world is connected. When you upset one thing in our environment, you can affect the environment many miles away.

GROW PLANTS FROM APPLE SEEDS

You can grow pretty green plants from apple seeds and other fruit seeds, such as pears, plums, peaches, and cherries. But first you must know a special fact about these seeds. Some seeds sprout right away when you plant them. But these fruit seeds do not. They need time to lie in the moist, cold soil during the winter. Changes take place in the seed during this time. The cold temperature causes chemical changes in the <u>embryo</u> (the "baby plant"). These changes make the seed start to <u>germinate</u>. Germinate means to start to develop. In the spring it is ready to sprout.

You can help the seed grow. You can make the seed think it is wintertime, even if it isn't. How? By putting it in the refrigerator. In a way you will be creating a "winter environment" for the seed.

Follow our instructions:

1. Take the seeds out of an apple. Wash and dry them. Then place them between two pieces of moist tissue in a jar.

2. Put the jar in the refrigerator. Keep the tissue moist, but not sopping wet. Feel it with your finger every few weeks to tell if it needs water. In about two months the seeds will have little green sprouts. Now you are ready to plant the seeds.

3. Put soil in a container with pebbles at the bottom for drainage. Make a little hole in the soil and put the sprout in the hole. Don't plant the sprout too deep. Just cover the roots with soil.

4. Put the container in a sunny window. Water the sprouts and soil only when the soil feels dry to the touch.

5. Keep the soil moist. Soon you will have a pretty little green plant. Watch your plant while it grows. How long does it take to develop? What does it look like while it is growing?

You can plant seeds from pears, plums, peaches, and cherries this way. But lemon, orange, grapefruit, and avocado seeds do not need this cold treatment. They grow better in a warm environment.

MORE APPLE ACTIVITIES

1. Apple trees aren't just found in apple orchards. Some small apple trees can be found in the city. The flowering crab apple, for example, is a good tree for backyards and small parks. Take a walk around your neighborhood. Can you find any apple trees? Call the Parks Department, Horticultural Society, or Botanical Garden. Ask where you can find apple trees in your city.

2. Does your school have an area where you can plant trees or flowers? A good project for a class or ecology club would be to plant an apple tree. You could take care of it and watch it bloom each year.

3. Trees are an important part of our environment. They are all different. But each tree is part of a community of living things. You can learn more about trees and how many living things depend on them for life. Read <u>Because of a Tree</u> by Lorus and Margery Milne (Atheneum, New York). One of the chapters is called "Around the Apple Tree." You'll enjoy this book. You can also read about other trees, such as sugar maples, Christmas trees, and palm trees.

4. Another book that would be fun to read is <u>The Hole in the Tree</u> by Jean George (E. P. Dutton & Co., New York). This is an adventure story. Read it and find out how the hole was started, how it got bigger, who used it as a home, how Scot and Paula found it and its treasures. Of course, the hole is in an apple tree! This book also shows how a tree is part of a community of living things.

5. Read "Pesticides Are Perilous." This is a reprint from <u>Ranger Rick's Nature Magazine</u>. It tells you what pesticides are and what they do. It gives you ideas on how to use "natural" controls instead. <u>Single</u> copies of this reprint are free. Write to the Educational Services Section, National Wildlife Federation, 1412 Sixteenth St., N.W., Washington, D.C. 20036.

6. Rodale Press, Inc. publishes a magazine called Organic Gardening and Farming. It also publishes many newsletters and books about the environment. Write to Rodale Press for information about organic apples and how they are grown. Also ask about companies that sell ladybugs and other natural insect controls. Send a stamped, self-addressed envelope with your request. Write to Rodale Press, Inc., Emmaus, Pa. 18049. (Ask your librarian to subscribe to one of their newsletters. They are very good.)

7. Visit a supermarket. Find out about the apples and apple products sold there. Here are some ideas.

     Make a list of all the different kinds of apples. Compare the looks of the apples you find. Compare the apples for flavor. Find out where the apples came from. Were any grown by organic methods? Were pesticides used? Did any apples have wax put on the outside to make them look shinier?

     Look for food products made from apples. Find frozen apple turnovers, apple juice, apple cider, apple pie filling, jelly apples, and cereal with apples. Read the labels on these foods very carefully. Make a list of the chemicals they contain.

8. Organic foods are foods that do not contain added chemicals. Sometimes they are called "natural foods." Visit a store that sells organic foods. Ask questions about how the foods are grown and processed.

CHAPTER TWENTY ONE

City Farming

When the weather changes, our environment changes. Wintertime in a city can be a gloomy time. There is less sunshine during winter's short days. Everything seems gray and dull. The wind blows through tree branches that have lost all their leaves. The parks aren't full of green grass or pretty flowers anymore. Most people are eager for spring to return. They want to see green again.

You can help put a little green into the city in the winter and brighten up your home at the same time. Remember, your environment is everything around you. That includes the place where you live. Wouldn't it be nice to walk into your house or apartment and see pretty green plants all year round?

You don't have to be a country person to have green plants. You don't have to have a "green thumb." You don't have to have a lot of money. All you need are a few simple supplies. Then give your plants lots of TLC (that's Tender Loving Care).

Read on. Learn how to grow a cheerful window garden from vegetable parts and fruit seeds.

Have fun. Happy planting.

WHAT YOUR PLANTS NEED TO HELP
THEM GROW

Soil

You can buy a package of soil for your plant at a seed dealer or garden store. This soil is especially mixed for plants growing in pots. It will hold water longer and has plant foods mixed in. You can learn how to mix your own special soil for your plants. Read one of the books we tell you about in this chapter.

Sun

Indoor plants should be put near sunny windows. They need the light from the sun to grow. Turn the plant every day. If you don't do this, the plant will not grow straight. It will lean toward the sun.

Water

Plants need water to live. But you must be very careful when you water plants. Too much water can kill them. The soil should be damp but not very wet or muddy. Try not to water the leaves. Water the soil, not the leaves.

Don't Let Plants Drown

There is something you can do to make sure that the soil does not get too wet. Put a hole in the bottom of your container so that the extra water can drain out. Then put bits of broken clay pots or a layer of pebbles over the hole. Now the water will drain out slowly. You can also cover the hole with half of an orange or grapefruit skin. Put a small pan or dish under the container to catch the water when it drains out.

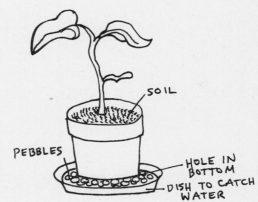

Sometimes you can grow a plant in water, instead of soil. Of course, you don't want holes in the bottom of your container then!

159

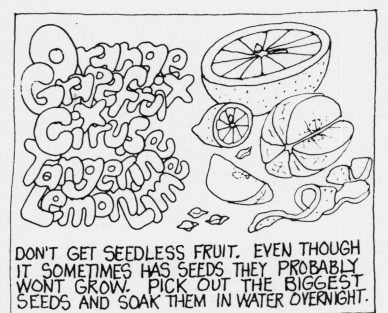

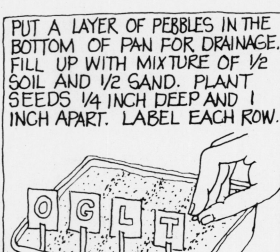

DON'T GET SEEDLESS FRUIT. EVEN THOUGH IT SOMETIMES HAS SEEDS THEY PROBABLY WONT GROW. PICK OUT THE BIGGEST SEEDS AND SOAK THEM IN WATER OVERNIGHT.

PUT A LAYER OF PEBBLES IN THE BOTTOM OF PAN FOR DRAINAGE. FILL UP WITH MIXTURE OF ½ SOIL AND ½ SAND. PLANT SEEDS ¼ INCH DEEP AND 1 INCH APART. LABEL EACH ROW.

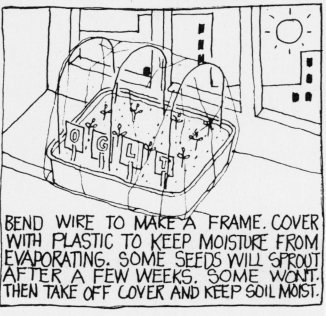

BEND WIRE TO MAKE A FRAME. COVER WITH PLASTIC TO KEEP MOISTURE FROM EVAPORATING. SOME SEEDS WILL SPROUT AFTER A FEW WEEKS. SOME WONT. THEN TAKE OFF COVER AND KEEP SOIL MOIST.

MOVE THE LARGER SEEDLINGS TO POTS. THEY WILL GROW BIGGER AND MAY HAVE SWEET-SMELLING FLOWERS AFTER A WHILE.

SUPPLIES

Here is a list of supplies you will need for the projects in this chapter. You won't need all these supplies for every project. Read the directions carefully <u>before</u> you get your supplies together.

Knife	Toothpicks	Wire
Spoon or fork to mix the soil	String	Plastic
	Soil	Many containers
Sticks for labeling seedlings (Ice cream sticks are good.)	Pebbles	

160

FRESH CARROTS TASTE GOOD AND THEY'RE GOOD FOR YOU TOO. BUT DID YOU KNOW THAT THE CARROT TOPS YOUR MOTHER THROWS AWAY CAN BECOME PRETTY PLANTS WITH DELICATE FEATHERY FOLIAGE

CUT OFF MOST OF THE LEAVES IF THERE ARE ANY. CUT OFF ABOUT 2 INCHES OF THE TOP OF THE CARROT.

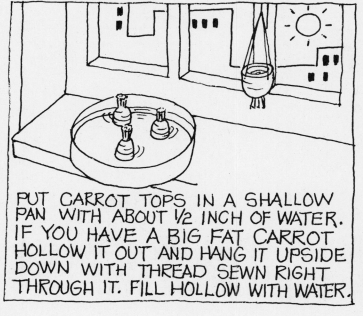

PUT CARROT TOPS IN A SHALLOW PAN WITH ABOUT ½ INCH OF WATER. IF YOU HAVE A BIG FAT CARROT HOLLOW IT OUT AND HANG IT UPSIDE DOWN WITH THREAD SEWN RIGHT THROUGH IT. FILL HOLLOW WITH WATER.

IF WATER GETS CLOUDY, CHANGE IT. WHEN CARROT TOPS GROW ROOTS YOU CAN MOVE THEM TO A PAN WITH MOIST SAND.

ECOLOGICAL CONTAINERS

You don't have to spend a lot of money for containers for your plants. You can make your own from things you usually throw away. Reusing things instead of putting them in the garbage helps the environment, too. Here are some ideas.

Plastic food containers (ice cream and margarine come in these)

Coffee cans

Old muffin tins

Plastic egg cartons

Pretzel and potato chip cans for large plants

Aluminum pans from frozen foods

CUT AVOCADO IN HALF AND TAKE OUT THE SEED.

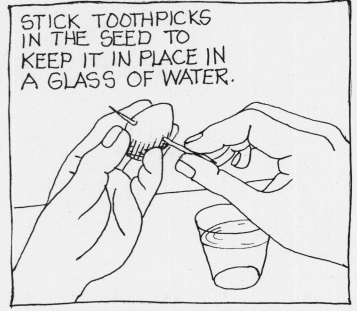

STICK TOOTHPICKS IN THE SEED TO KEEP IT IN PLACE IN A GLASS OF WATER.

PLACE SEED ON GLASS POINTED END UP. THE BOTTOM OF SEED MUST BE IN WATER. IN ABOUT 3 OR 4 WEEKS A WHITE ROOT WILL GROW FROM BOTTOM OF SEED. WHEN ROOT IS 2 OR 3 INCHES LONG...

REMOVE TOOTHPICKS AND MOVE TO A POT WITH SOIL. PLANT SEED HALF UNDER SOIL. SOON TOP OF SEED WILL CRACK OPEN AND A GREEN SHOOT WILL COME OUT.

LEARN MORE ABOUT PLANTS

Read <u>Plants to Grow Indoors</u> by George Sullivan (Follett Publishing Company, Chicago). This book is for younger readers. It will show you how to mix your own soil for your plants. There are lots of projects to teach you more about plants and how they live. You can learn how to grow many different kinds of house plants. There are lots of pictures and the instructions are very easy to understand.

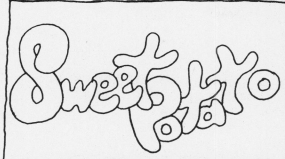

YOU CAN GROW A BEAUTIFUL VINE TO HANG FROM THE TOP OF A WINDOW OR PUT ON A WINDOWSILL.
WHAT DO YOU NEED TO GROW THIS VINE?
A SWEET POTATO!

SOMETIMES SWEET POTATOES SOLD IN SUPERMARKETS ARE TREATED TO KEEP THEM FROM SPROUTING.

ONE UNTREATED SWEET POTATO PLEASE

TRY TO GET AN UNTREATED ONE. IF YOU CAN'T, TRY TO REMOVE THE TREATMENT BY SCRUBBING.

STICK TOOTHPICKS IN TO KEEP IT IN PLACE.

START SWEET POTATO IN A GLASS OF WATER POINTED END DOWN.

WHEN THE GREEN SHOOTS ARE A FEW INCHES LONG MOVE TO A POT WITH SOIL.

THIS IS HOW IT WILL LOOK AFTER 1 YEAR.

LEARN MORE ABOUT PLANTS

Read Plants for Pots by D.X. Fenten (J.B. Lippincott Company, New York). This book is full of information about indoor gardening. You'll learn how to grow plants from seeds and from other plants. You'll learn how to grow your own miniature peach tree and vegetables or herbs for your kitchen table. There is a special section about unusual plants. Some of them eat insects, grow piggyback, or are sensitive to touch. The last part of the book has projects for each month for home and school. It gives great ideas for growing plants for special holidays and for gifts.

GROW A BEAUTIFUL PLANT FROM
A PINEAPPLE TOP

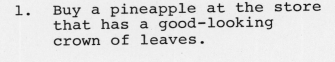

1. Buy a pineapple at the store that has a good-looking crown of leaves.

2. Slice off the top with a sharp knife. Cut it where the leaves join the pineapple, but leave a little of the pineapple. Take off the lower three rows of leaves. Dry out the pineapple top for a few days.

3. Then plant it in sand about 1/4 of an inch deep. The best kind of sand to use is "builder's sand." Find a building that is going up. Ask if you can have a little sand for your container. If you use ocean beach sand, wash it first to get the salt out.

4. Keep the sand damp. Keep the pot out of the sun until the leaves start to grow. Now you can move the plant to a pot with soil.

5. Then put the plant in a sunny window. Water the plant from the top. If you are lucky, the plant might get pretty blue flowers. In pineapple plants, the flowers grow together and form a pineapple. This will probably not happen in your plant, though.

HERB GARDENS

Have you ever seen an herb garden? You may
have thought it was a bunch of weeds. But these
weed-like plants have many uses, and people have
been raising them for centuries.

In long-ago times, herbs were used by everybody for medicine and flavoring. Some herbs were
also used to <u>preserve</u> food; that is, to make it
last a long time without spoiling. When people
moved from place to place, they were always sure
to take herb seeds or plants with them so they
could have them in the new home.

HERBS

About 100 years ago, herbs began to
be used less and less. People invented
other ways of preserving food. They
made artificial flavors and began to
discover new kinds of medicines. They
almost forgot about herbs.

Now a lot of people are using herbs again.
They are learning again that herbs can be helpful for good taste and good health.

Why not raise some herbs? See for yourself
how good your food can taste with these natural
flavorings. Make a tea from special herbs. And
learn about gardening the easy way.

Herbs can be easily raised in a backyard garden or
in containers on sunny windowsills. Most herbs do best
in <u>light</u> soil that doesn't have too much <u>clay</u>. (You can
test the soil by picking some up and squeezing it in your
hand. If the ball of earth crumbles when you let it go,
the soil is light and <u>sandy</u>.) Herbs should have <u>well-
drained</u> soil, where water does not collect in puddles.
They grow best in full sunlight.

You can raise herbs from seeds that you buy from catalogues. You can also buy seeds at plant and hardware stores. Or ask adult herb gardeners to give you small parts of their own growing plants. These are called <u>shoots</u>.

If you don't have an outdoor garden, you can put herbs in small containers, such as juice cans. Each herb should be planted in a separate can. Punch holes in the bottom of each can. Add a layer of pebbles. Then add soil made of 1/3 <u>potting soil</u>, 1/3 <u>coarse sand</u>, and 1/3 <u>vermiculite</u>. Ask for these by name at plant or hardware stores. Or your parents and their friends may be able to give you some.

Plant either seeds or shoots in your garden in a sunny, well-drained spot. Or put containers on a sunny windowsill. Don't water them too much.

After the seeds begin to grow, you will have too many plants for the space. So you must thin them by pulling some out to leave more room for the others. Transfer the plants you pulled out to another container or another part of the garden. As the plants in containers get bigger, you will have to put them in larger pots.

Here are five herbs that you can grow. Since they are all <u>perennial</u> plants, they will come back year after year.

1. <u>Lavender</u> is dried and put in drawers to make clothes smell good.
2. <u>Peppermint</u> makes a good tea to help tummy-aches.
3. <u>Oregano</u> is tasty in pizza.
4. <u>Rosemary</u> can be sprinkled on baked potatoes.
5. <u>Thyme</u> is delicious on green peas.

CHAPTER TWENTY TWO

Gardens in Glass

City people rarely see natural places unless they visit a large park or botanical garden. They often don't have backyards where they can grow their own gardens. They miss the fun of choosing and planting the plants they like, then watching them grow.

That's why many city people like to grow gardens in windows. They also love terrariums. A terrarium is a miniature garden growing in a covered glass container. It fits easily into a home or classroom.

The idea for terrariums developed by accident. In 1829, the English scientist Nathanial Ward put an insect on some soil in a bottle. Later, he saw a fern growing in the moist soil. He was very surprised. He knew ferns could not grow in London. The air was too polluted from the factories. But Dr. Ward's little fern was protected from this harmful air by the closed bottle. It sprouted and lived a healthy four years.

Dr. Ward then started growing many other interesting plants in containers. These glass gardens became very popular in homes. They were called "Wardian cases."

What is a terrarium today? It is no longer a "Wardian case," but nearly any garden under glass. For example, a desert terrarium is an arrangement of plants that need dryness and lots of sunshine. A marsh scene is made of plants that like to be kept moist. And a woodland terrarium is made of plants that like coolness and only a little sun.

WHY MAKE A TERRARIUM?

They Decorate a Room

Terrariums are little gardens in glass containers. They decorate city apartments and make them seem cheerier. The containers frame the gardens just like a painting.

You Can Use Your Imagination

What kinds of plants would you like in your terrarium? You can choose from many different kinds of plants. You can choose the sizes, shapes, and colors that please you. Then you can arrange them in the way you like best.

Containers are as much fun to choose as the plants. They come in hundreds of sizes and shapes. You can pick the one that looks nicest in your room.

They're Easy to Take Care Of

In a closed container, moisture cannot escape to the air. So you don't have to water the plants very often.

Plants Are Protected in Terrariums

Sometimes it is hard for plants to live in city buildings. There is a lot of pollution. Many plants don't like the dry air of steam-heated apartments and classrooms.

Terrariums protect plants from dry air and pollution. In a closed container, plants are also protected from harmful insects. And they are protected from drafts and other changes in temperature.

WHAT CAN YOU LEARN FROM OBSERVING A TERRARIUM?

A terrarium is a closed world. It is like a little world all by itself. Plants have all they need to live inside the container. By studying a terrarium you can learn more about how plants live.

Plants need food. They need light. They need carbon dioxide and oxygen. They need soil and water. In a terrarium, plants get the ingredients they need for all their activities.

1. <u>Learn About the Water Cycle</u>--
A terrarium stays wet for a long time. You don't have to water it often. This is because the water never leaves the container. It is used over and over again.

First, the water is used as a liquid by the plants. Some of the unused water evaporates and becomes water vapor. The terrarium glass is usually cooler than the water vapor. On the glass the water vapor will become liquid water again. This is called <u>condensation</u>.

2. <u>Learn About Plant Behavior</u>--Plants need sunlight to make their food. Many times they will turn to follow the sun. If you place a terrarium in different positions, you will see the plants turn to face the sun.

3. <u>Learn About Photosynthesis</u>--When plants use sunlight to make their food it is called <u>photosynthesis</u>. They get energy from the sun. They get carbon dioxide from the air. They get water from the soil. Plants use these things to make sugars for food. They return oxygen and moisture from their leaves to the air. Plants in a terrarium, like all plants, use sunlight to make food.

Try an experiment. Cover a small plant with a cup. It will get everything it needs except sunlight. In a day or two take a look at it. Is it still green? Did it grow? Can you explain what happened?

PLANNING YOUR TERRARIUM

What Equipment Will You Need?

Get everything you need before you start planting your terrarium.

1. Clear glass containers will let you see your plants easily. Containers with wide openings are the easiest to use. You should be able to fit your hands inside them. It is hard to get plants and soil into containers with skinny openings unless you have tools. Use wide-mouth jars like gallon-size mayonnaise, peanut butter or pickle jars. Or use goldfish bowls, or aquariums. Save your container tops. Or get a clear piece of plastic or glass to use as a cover.

2. You will also need gravel, sand, charcoal, peat moss, and potting soil. How much you will need depends on the size of your container.

PEAT MOSS POTTING SOIL GRAVEL SAND CHARCOAL

3. Wood chips, bits of branches, pebbles, small colored rocks, or shells will help decorate your terrarium and make it look like a natural setting.

Where Will You Get Everything?

Making a terrarium doesn't have to be expensive. Use a container you find at home or that a neighbor or relative can give to you. You can buy your plants, soil, and charcoal from a dime store or plant store. (Dime stores are cheaper.) Or use plants that are already growing at home.

Prayer Plant

Begonia

What Plants Should You Use?

It isn't easy for city dwellers to obtain wild plants. But they can get cultivated plants. Begonias, ferns, prayer plants, African violets, and ivy are cultivated plants. They can be bought in dime stores, flower shops, or supermarkets. Your terrarium will be called a cultivated terrarium.

Many of these plants prefer the environment of a terrarium. It is always moist and warm. If it is not too heavy, bring your container with you when you purchase your plants. You can see how many will fit into the size and shape of the container. Choose plants with different heights, shapes, and patterns. Variety will make your terrarium more interesting.

170

PLANTING YOUR TERRARIUM

1. Wash your container thoroughly in hot water to make sure it is clean. Also wash anything you pick up from the ground to decorate your container.

2. Place 1 inch or a little less gravel at the bottom of the container. This lets the extra water drain from the soil so the soil won't be soggy.

POTTING SOIL, PEAT MOSS, SAND
CHARCOAL
GRAVEL

3. Cover the gravel with a thin layer of charcoal. The charcoal holds oxygen in the soil and keeps the soil fresh.

4. Moisten the potting soil, sand, and peat moss. Combine equal amounts of each. The sand helps drainage. The peat moss helps to nourish the soil and keeps it moist. Put about 2 inches of the mixture into the container. Add more of the planting mix in some places so there will be small hills and valleys, just as you would see in a natural landscape.

5. Poke holes about 1 inch deep in your planting mix. Remove the plants you are going to use from their pots. Carefully push off the excess dirt from the roots.

6. Put the plants in the holes. Replace the soil around them. Be sure not to crowd your plants. Try not to push them against the walls of the container.

A square container looks pretty with large plants in the back and smaller ones up front. In a round container, try putting the largest plant in the center and the small ones around it.

7. Dress up your terrarium with things you would find in nature, such as rocks and shells.

8. Cover the container.

9. Remember that terrariums keep their moisture because they are closed containers. Be careful not to overwater them. Water the garden gently with a sprinkler. Some water cans have sprinklers attached. Or at a dime store you can buy a rubber sprinkler used to moisten clothes for ironing.

TAKING CARE OF YOUR TERRARIUM

1. Keep it in good light but not in direct sunlight. Too much sun will burn most terrarium plants.

2. Water it only about once a month, or whenever the soil dries out.

3. If the container gets foggy, there is too much moisture. Remove the cover until the excess moisture evaporates.

4. Remove all dead leaves. Trim overgrown plants. Do this by cutting the leaves where they meet the stem of the plants.

OTHER USES FOR TERRARIUMS

1. Large terrariums make good plant hospitals or nursing homes. Sick house plants often recover when they are kept for a while in the humid atmosphere of a terrarium.

2. Large terrariums can be used as greenhouses. Here plants can be grown in their pots. Cover the terrarium floor with a couple of inches of gravel or sand. Water the gravel, and insert the plant pots. Use plant pots that have holes in the bottom. This is where water from the gravel or sand will enter the plants.

3. Terrariums can serve as nurseries or maternity wards. Here seeds will sprout. Cuttings from plants will take root. Baby plants will grow up.

4. Who will water your plants when you go on vacation? Save large clear plastic bags. You can use them to cover groups of plants while you are away. This will create the environment and conditions of a terrarium. The recycled moisture will take care of your plants. Put tall sticks in the soil to hold the plastic up like a tent and keep the plastic from touching the leaves.

MORE GARDENS UNDER GLASS

A terrarium isn't the only kind of garden you can have under glass. A <u>vivarium</u> is like a terrarium but it contains animals as well as plants. You can also have a <u>sealed world</u>. That's like a vivarium, but it also contains water and fish. Each little world shows how living things interact with their environment. (You can learn how to make a <u>sealed world</u> in chapter two of this book).

VIVARIUMS

In a vivarium, plants and small animals live together. You usually have to help feed the animals in a small vivarium. But in a large vivarium, plants and animals can have all they need to live together. Then it is a complete closed little world.

What Do You Find in a Vivarium?

A vivarium has rocks, soil, air, and water. These are the non-living things. Then there are plants, and insects that live among the plants. The vivarium also has little animals such as frogs, toads, turtles, salamanders, and snails. Because a vivarium is covered, like a terrarium, it does not need to be watered often.

A Vivarium Shows Nature's Cycle

Everything in the vivarium takes part in a cycle of nature. Soil, water, and air nourish the plants. Insects eat the plants for food. Then the little animals eat the insects. When leaves die, bacteria help <u>decompose</u> them. Bacteria break down the fallen leaves into little <u>particles</u> that enrich the soil. The plants take their food from the soil, and the cycle begins again.

LEARN MORE BY YOURSELF

Call or write to your local botanical garden. Ask if they have information or classes on terrariums.

Do some reading on terrariums and vivariums. One good book is <u>Terrariums</u> by John Hoke (Franklin Watts, 1972). It is for older readers and describes different types of terrariums. The book also tells you where to order plants and equipment.

Another good book, and this one is for younger readers, is <u>Small Habitats</u> by Lilo Hess (Charles Scribner's Sons, 1976). You will learn all about vivariums and how to set up your own. The book contains many photographs to show what different kinds of vivariums should look like.

173

CHAPTER TWENTY THREE

Weather Report

How do we know what kind of day it is? Our eyesight tells us when it's sunny. We hear the rain. With our sense of touch, we feel how hot or cold it is. What are our senses describing to us? They are describing the weather.

Many different things go together to make weather. Can you have rain without clouds? Can there be a hurricane without winds? Will a day be hot and bright without the sun? Sun, wind, clouds, rain--all are a part of the weather that affects our lives every day.

We can't ignore the weather. Often it forces us to change our plans. When it's very cold, we can't play outdoors. Ballgames are sometimes "rained out." Airports can be closed because of fog. Even whole cities can be shut down by a hurricane.

Weather affects people, but people also affect the weather. When many people live close together in cities, they cause great changes in the natural things around them. Weather is one of the natural things that has been changed by city life.

This chapter is all about weather and the city. As you read it, you will begin to understand how weather happens, how it affects people's lives, and how people are affecting weather.

WHAT MAKES HEAT?

The most important thing about weather
is <u>heat</u>. We measure heat by taking its
<u>temperature</u> with a thermometer. The more
heat, the higher the temperature. We feel
much warmer when the thermometer measures
90°F. than when it measures 30°F.

Heat is a form of energy. Like all other
energy, it comes from the sun. The sun's hot
gases give off heat energy and light energy.
Between the earth and the sun is a great distance
of empty space, called a <u>vacuum</u>. Heat energy
cannot travel directly across a vacuum. But
light energy (sunlight) can easily cross the
vacuum and change to heat energy after it gets
to our earth.

When sunlight reaches the earth, some
of it is bounced away by <u>reflection</u>. Sunlight
is reflected by shiny or light-colored surfaces.
Think of the white sand at the beach. Doesn't
the sunlight look especially bright at the
beach?

Some sunlight is <u>not</u> reflected away from earth. It is
<u>absorbed</u> into the ground or water. Then its light energy
changes to heat energy. This is how the sunlight warms our
earth.

HOW DOES HEAT MAKE WEATHER?

The heat from the sun causes the earth's
air and water to change temperature and move.
When air becomes warm, it rises. You've
probably sometimes noticed the warm moving
air rippling above a fire or hot radiator.

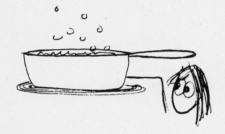

Warm water also moves. You've seen
it in a pan of water on the stove. As
the liquid in the pan heats up, it
bubbles. Some of it changes to rising
steam, or <u>vapor</u>.

Warm, moving air creates
winds. Winds blow in certain
directions because some parts
of the earth warm up faster
than other parts. During the
day, the seashore heats up more
quickly than the ocean. The
air above the land becomes warm
and rises. The cooler air over
the ocean moves toward the land
to take the place of the warmer
air. So ocean breeezes are created.

Other, bigger winds often begin at
the hottest part of the earth--the
<u>equator</u>. There, direct sunlight makes
the air very warm. The air rises and
moves toward the North and South Poles.
The poles, as you know, receive the
least amount of direct sunlight. Their
cold air moves toward the equator to
replace the warm, rising air. So the
earth's winds move around the world by
the energy of heat.

When the earth's water absorbs
the sun's heat, some of it becomes so
warm that it changes from liquid into
vapor, just as in the pan of heated
water on your stove. As the warm vapor
rises, there will be less liquid left.
This is called <u>evaporation</u>.

The warm air that rises begins to cool. Its water vapor
changes back to liquid. This is <u>condensation</u>. You can see
condensation at work when hot air hits a cold window--there
will be a film of water on the glass.

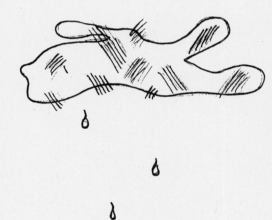

Water vapor condenses into dust
and dirt specks that float in the air.
The water droplets that are formed
collect together to become clouds.
When enough droplets have joined
together, they can become heavy enough
to fall as rain.

Often the temperature in the clouds is below freezing. The
cloud droplets freeze to form tiny ice crystals. When the crystals
join, snow is made. If the air temperature between the clouds and
the ground is below freezing, snow will fall.

If you are ever on the top floors of a skyscraper, you may
observe an interesting thing. The air is colder there than it is
at street level. So people who work on the top floors may see
snow falling that will be melted into rain by the time it reaches
the street.

HOW DO CITIES "MAKE" WEATHER?

Cities can affect their weather by making it hotter.

In large cities, many machines are used to make, move, heat, or cool things. As machines use energy, they produce a lot of waste heat. So cities become <u>heat</u> <u>islands</u>. They are much warmer than the countryside where there are fewer machines. Listen to the weather reporters on TV or radio. Almost always, the temperature in cities is slightly higher than in the country.

There is another reason why cities are hotter. As cities grow, they replace forests and fields with asphalt and concrete. Asphalt streets and concrete sidewalks absorb more sunlight than forests and fields do. Then they become like ovens, giving off their heat for hours, especially at night.

Since cities are heat islands, they are sources of warm, moist air. As this air rises and cools, it forms cloud droplets around the many dirt specks of the cities' polluted air. So cities may have more cloudy weather than the country.

Some scientists think that large cities act as "rainmakers" for places near them. It has been found that the rainfall is heavier in places that receive the winds from large cities. Can you explain how this could happen?

HOW DOES WEATHER AFFECT AIR POLLUTION?

Weather can help cities get rid of air pollution. Most of our air pollution is produced in large cities, and the air in many places is getting dirtier all the time. Winds can help remove air pollution. They can blow away air that has become dirty from pollution.

The winds also force the pollution to mix with the cleaner air the winds bring in. This reduces the amount of air pollution there is in one place.

While the winds remove air pollution from the cities, the rain washes the winds. The rain captures the soot and gases and carries them to the ground. This makes the winds much cleaner, but it may make the rain very dirty.

Sometimes the weather can make air pollution far worse. This is what happens during a <u>temperature inversion</u>. In normal times, cold air from above mixes with warm air from below. This keeps the air moving and helps to clean it. But when an inversion comes, warm air sits on top of the cooler air and keeps it from moving. Then pollution is trapped in the cooler air at the ground. Air pollution can become very bad and people will sometimes get sick.

YOU CAN BE A WEATHER OBSERVER

Understanding the weather is sometimes difficult. Try some of the experiments below. They will help you remember some of the things you have learned about the weather.

1. Measure Reflection and Absorption of Sunlight

Materials needed: Five thermometers

Leave one thermometer on a sidewalk, one under a tree, one on a sunny lawn, one in a sandbox, and one in a large bowl of water placed outside. Let them stay in place for an hour. What temperature does the thermometer measure at each place? Which places have cool temperatures? Which places are the warmest? What does this tell you about the reflection and absorption of sunlight?

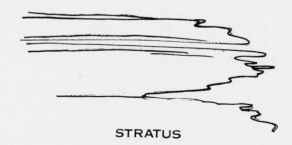

NOTE: Be sure to do all parts of this experiment on the same day.

2. Predict Weather from Clouds

Materials needed: Notebook and pencil

Observe the three types of clouds. You will see clouds that are heaped up (cumulus), clouds that are wispy (cirrus), and clouds in large sheets (stratus). Each type of cloud is caused by a different kind of weather. Keep a list of the clouds you see, a list of what the weather is when you see them, and a list of what the weather is two hours later. After two weeks, read what you have written. What do you notice? Could you start predicting what the day's weather will be by observing clouds?

CUMULUS

CIRRUS

STRATUS

180

3. Sample the Air

Materials needed: Piece of heavy paper and clear tape

Punch a hole in the middle of the piece of paper. Put a strip of clear tape under the hole. Make sure the sticky surface of the tape shows through the hole. Leave the paper outside for two days. Then look at it with a magnifying glass. What was caught on the tape? Sample the air in several different kinds of places. Do you catch the same things on the tape? Where does the air seem to be dirtiest?

This experiment was suggested in The Conservationist, a publication of the New York State Department of Conservation.

CHAPTER TWENTY FOUR

The Climate Question

When spring comes, the cold weather ends.
Even though the temperature will change from day
to day, we know that the next few months will be
warm ones. And we know that it will get cool
again in the fall.

Everybody notices the big weather
changes in a place. They may
say: "This place usually has cold weather."
"It rains too much here." "That city is
hot and dry all year round." When people
tell each other what the weather is like
over a long period of time, they are
talking about <u>climate</u>. Even though it is
hard to predict our weather from day to
day, we know what the climate will be in a
certain part of the country at a certain
season. It will be pretty much the same
year after year.

Most natural things live best in a particular climate. Palm
trees like hot climates. You wouldn't see them in a New York City
park where it is cold in winter. Polar bears like the cold and
don't live well in Florida where it is hot most of the time.
People can live almost anywhere, but they prefer climates that are
not too hot or too cold.

The kind of climate we have is one of
the most important things we notice about our
environment. But what makes climate? How does
climate affect people and cities? Could we
ever change our climate? This chapter
will help you find some answers to these
questions.

A JOURNEY THROUGH CLIMATES

If you were to take a trip around the world, you would pass through many different climates. Near the equator, you would probably be very warm. The tropical climates in this part of the world are hot. They never cool off.

In some tropical climates, it rains every day. We might call it "steambath climate." Other tropical climates have two seasons--wet and dry. Clothing and houses in tropical climates are built to keep out rain. But they don't have to protect people from cold.

On a helicopter ride to the North Pole, you would find cold polar climate. It never gets hot. Living there would be like living in your freezer.

At the poles, snow covers the ground all year and the waterways are usually frozen. You would find very few people living near these regions. Those who do must wear many layers of clothing to keep their bodies warm. Houses are built of snow blocks, because there is no other building material.

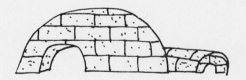

Most of your trip around the world would take you through the changeable climates between tropical and polar. These are called temperate climates, because they do not get extremely hot or extremely cold. We are all familiar with these climates because they are our climates.

Many plants and animals do well in temperate climates. As the four seasons-- spring, summer, winter, and fall--roll around each year, people can enjoy many different kinds of life. It is not hard to see why most of the world's people live in temperate climates.

THE SUN'S RAYS MAKE CLIMATES

In the chapter on weather, you learned that the energy of sunlight gives us the heat that makes weather. Since climate is made by the weather over a long period of time, sunlight is very important to climate, too.

We picture the earth as a ball, though it is not really round. (It is more oval, or pear-shaped.) At the equator, where the earth is biggest, the sun's rays strike head on. This is <u>direct</u> sunlight. Our hottest climates are where the sun's rays are direct.

At the North and South Poles the sun's rays strike to the side. This is <u>indirect</u> sunlight. Since the poles don't get a lot of heat energy from direct sunlight, they have the earth's coldest climates.

The changeable temperate climates take in both direct and indirect rays of the sun, depending on the time of year. This is because our earth is tilted. As the earth travels around the sun, the part of the earth north of the equator is tilted <u>toward</u> the sun and we have summer. The hot weather is from the sun's direct rays.

When South America, in the southern half of the earth, is tilted toward the sun, it will be summer there. At the same time, our part of the earth (the northern part) will be tilted away from the sun. The indirect rays of the sun will cause our winter.

The next time you are enjoying warm weather and outdoor life, think about the boys and girls in Argentina and Chile, who are bundled up in coats and gloves for the winter!

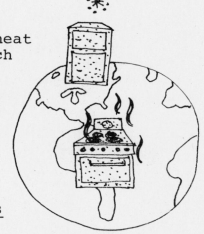

The equator receives enough heat energy from sunlight to make it much hotter than it actually is. Polar climate could also be much colder, especially during the long winters. What keeps the earth from turning into half-oven and half-freezer?

Winds

As you learned in reading about weather, warm air near the equator causes great winds to blow toward the North and South Poles. These winds help to spread the heat of the tropics to places that don't get as much heat from the sun. This makes the equator an important source of heat for other climates.

In turn, cold polar winds blow toward the equator and help to cool off the temperate and tropical climates. So the exchange of warm and cool winds helps to "air condition" the earth.

Currents

Ocean waters are also warmed in the tropics. Warm ocean currents flow toward the poles. Currents are like enormous rivers running in the sea. They make the nearby coasts much warmer. Even though Iceland is near the North Pole, the tropical current called the Gulf Stream makes the climate warmer there.

Cold ocean currents from the poles help to make temperate and tropical lands cooler and drier. Peru, which is near the equator, is affected in this way by the cold Humboldt Current from the South Pole waters.

CITIES AND CLIMATES

Early people moved around all the time, finding the climates they liked best. But, after a while, they settled down and began building towns and cities.

Climate was a very important reason for locating a town in a certain place. Early towns had to be built where climates were good for growing crops.

Although town and city people began to do many different jobs besides farming, they depended on the farmers for food. And farmers needed plenty of sunshine and water to grow crops.

Towns also needed water for drinking and washing. They had to be built in places with good rainfall, or near a river or lake. Sometimes there was not enough rain and there would be a <u>drought</u>. At other times, it rained too much. This would cause a <u>flood</u>. Climate and weather changes that cause flooding and drought have caused tremendous problems for towns and cities. Sometimes towns have even disappeared as a result!

In modern times, people in cities try to ignore the climate. They build houses with artificial climates made by heating and air conditioning. In order to do this, they use lots of energy. They burn fuel to heat buildings, and they use many kilowatts of electricity to cool them. In making artificial climates, modern cities have become dependent on energy.

What do you think would happen if we ran out of fuel to heat our buildings? What do people do in the hot summer when electricity shortages cause "brownouts" and "blackouts"? Should we keep on using so much energy to create our artificial climates?

ARE WE CHANGING THE EARTH'S CLIMATES?

Each year people take over more of the earth and change it for their own needs. Some scientists believe we are doing many things that could accidentally change the earth's climates. We could make climates cooler or warmer. If we <u>do</u> change the earth's climates, we will also change our lives.

As you know, the heat for our earth comes from the sun's energy passing through the earth's air. Two of the gases in the air are <u>carbon dioxide</u> (CO_2) and <u>water vapor</u>. These gases let sunlight <u>reach</u> our earth easily. But the gases also absorb a lot of the heat that escapes from the earth's surface.

The "Greenhouse Effect"

The air around the earth becomes a very good heat trap. Scientists call this the "greenhouse effect." The envelope of air around the earth can become very warm. Some of the heat energy in the air will then be released to the earth and make it hotter.

The more carbon dioxide (CO_2) there is in the air, the easier it is for the air to hold heat. Since we burn much more fuel today, we are producing more CO_2 than we used to. Some scientists believe we are making too much CO_2. They think the extra CO_2 in the air will cause the "greenhouse effect" to become much bigger. Then the earth's air will capture more heat energy. So the earth's climates may change and become warmer.

Cooling Off

Other scientists think we are <u>not</u> warming the earth's climates with our man-made activities. Instead, they think we may be making climates cooler. We send dirt and waste gases into the air from cars, jets, factories, and incinerators. This air pollution can block out sunlight and prevent us from getting as much heat as we would if our air were clean. This is what happens in many large cities.

Bad farming practices may also put more dirt and dust into the air. Land that is plowed may become <u>eroded</u>. This means that the good soil on top blows away. The dirt and dust stay up in the air for years. This, too, can block out sunlight.

If sunlight is prevented from reaching the earth, we will receive less heat energy. World temperatures may fall. And the earth's climates may begin to cool.

Who Is Right?

Are climates becoming warmer or cooler? We don't know <u>which</u> scientists are really right. The <u>information</u> from people who are studying clouds shows us just how confused it all is.

You remember that both heat and dust help to form clouds. As more clouds form, they can have two effects on the climate. Since clouds are made of water vapor, they help create the "greenhouse effect" by capturing and holding the earth's heat energy. In this way, they can make the world hotter.

But clouds also reflect away a lot of sunlight. This is sunlight that would have given us heat. So, in this way, clouds may cause the world to become cooler.

You can see that even the greatest scientists in the world find it difficult to understand climate completely!

DO YOUR OWN THINKING ABOUT CLIMATE

Scientists are making some good guesses
about climate. Why don't you make a few guesses
of your own? Can you guess what would happen to
the earth's climate if:

1. All the clouds in the sky disappeared?

2. The ice at the North and South Poles melted?

3. Everybody in the world used cars for trans-
    portation?

4. Water could not absorb heat energy from
    sunlight?

Discuss your answers with your teachers and classmates.

CHAPTER TWENTY FIVE

Exploring the Seashore Environment

Do you live near the sea-shore? Or do you ever visit the seashore during vacations?

The environment of the sea-shore is very special. You can learn a great deal by exploring the beaches and water.

In this chapter we give lots of suggestions about things to collect at the beach and experiments to do with the things you find.

Have you ever made pretty designs with beach glass? Have you ever taken a really close look at sand? When was the last time you made a picture with seaweed?

These are just a few ideas to help you learn from the sea-shore environment. And while you are learning, you'll have a wonderful time.

BE A SEASHORE COLLECTOR

People collect many things that are found at the beach. Some collect seashells. Some collect pretty stones. Others collect driftwood that comes in all shapes and sizes.

Beach glass is also fun to collect. Beach glass is left over from man's garbage. It is usually from broken soda bottles.

You've seen broken glass before in vacant lots and on the street. The sharp, jagged edges are dangerous. But something happens to broken glass when it is in the sand and sea for a long time. The sharp edges get smooth. The glass changes color. It gets frosty. This glass is called beach glass.

Lots of people like to collect beach glass because it is so pretty. You can do a lot of things with it. Just use your imagination. Here's one idea.

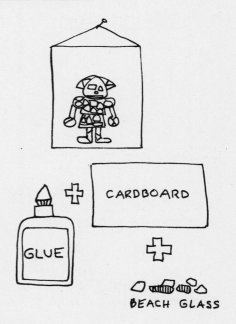

CARDBOARD

GLUE

BEACH GLASS

Make a design on a piece of old cardboard. Cut out the design. Put glue on the cardboard. Then glue the glass chips to the cardboard. Hang it up with a piece of string.

Be very careful when you make your glass collection. Remember, collect only smooth pieces of beach glass.

LEARN MORE BY YOURSELF

We found a wonderful book to help you find treasure at the beach. It will give you ideas for projects with shells, beach glass, pebbles, and many other things. It is called The Beachcomber's Book. It was written by Bernice Cohn and her instructions are very easy to follow. Ask for this book at your library. The publisher is The Viking Press.

BUILDING A WATER SNOOPERSCOPE

Learn more about what's going on under the water with a
Water Snooperscope. You can build it yourself and have lots
of fun.

What Do You Need to Build a Water Snooperscope?

If the water is shallow enough for you to stand in, you
will only need a short snooperscope. If you have to lean over
a dock or a boat, you will need a long snooperscope. Here are
the materials you should have to build both kinds of snooperscopes.

Short Snooperscope   You will need a big tin can like the ones
                      fruit juices come in. Remove the top and bottom.

Long Snooperscope   You will need a big piece of pipe that is at
                      least 3 feet long. Ask a grown-up where you
                      can get a piece of old, clean stovepipe or
                      a piece of ventilating system pipe. Maybe
                      you can get a piece from a junkyard.

Both Snooperscopes   You will need:

                      A clear plastic bag that is big enough to fit
                      over one end of your can or pipe

                      Two large heavy rubber bands

                      Strong, waterproof plastic tape

How Do You Put It Together?

First you have to put tape around
both ends of the can or pipe so you
won't cut yourself on the sharp edges.

Then you put the plastic bag over
one end of the scope. Make sure the
plastic bag fits tightly and smoothly up
against the opening, or it will be hard
to see through the scope. Hold the bag in
place by putting one of the rubber bands
around the scope about an inch from the edge.
Put the second rubber band around the scope
near the top edge of the plastic bag.

CAN OR PIPE · RUBBER BANDS · PLASTIC BAG

Put the end of the scope that has plastic around it under
the water. Look through the other end, and see what you find!

We learned about the Water Snooperscope from the Massachusetts
Audubon Society in Lincoln, Massachusetts.

DO EXPERIMENTS WITH SEA SALT

Did you ever swallow ocean water while you were swimming? Was it salty? How did the salt get there?

Salt and other minerals are in the soil. Rain washes the salt into streams and rivers. These streams and rivers flow into the ocean. Water evaporates from the ocean on hot days. But the salt stays right where it is.

Bring some sea water home with you in a covered jar. Boil it in a pot on the stove. When the water is all gone, look at the bottom of the pot. Salt will be left on the bottom. Salt from the ocean is a mixture of many different kinds of salts.

Sometimes the ocean waves throw pieces of wood onto the beach. The water evaporates from this driftwood, but the salt stays. When the driftwood is burned, you can see many different colors in the fire. These colors are the salts burning. Some of the flames might be orange. Others might be green, red, or blue. Different kinds of salt make different colors in the fire.

Many living things in the ocean contain salt. Burn some shells. Be very careful when you do this. Do you see any colors in the flames?

LEARN MORE BY YOURSELF

Do you like to explore new places? You can make many discoveries at the seashore. See Along the Shore is a good book to help you make these discoveries. You can learn how animals and plants in the sea use salts. You can find out how many living things live in the sand. You can learn more about tides. Read this book before you go to the beach. Then look for the many things it describes. See Along the Shore is by Millicent E. Selsam (Harper & Row, New York).

193

MAKE DISCOVERIES IN SAND

Most boys and girls enjoy
playing in the sand at the beach.
But did you ever wonder where the
sand came from? Millions of years
ago tiny pieces of rock broke off
the sides of mountains. The rain
washed them into streams and rivers.
Finally they reached the ocean.
And the ocean waves washed these tiny
pieces of rock--or sand--onto the
beach.

Grains of sand come from many different rocks. So they are
not all alike. Some are heavier than others. Most are white,
yellow, or gray. They come from a stone called granite. But
some are reddish brown, black, pink, or other colors. Sometimes,
along a mountain stream, you can even find yellow grains that
are real gold!

Investigate for yourself. Bring with you a <u>spoon</u>, a <u>shallow
pan</u> (cake pan), a <u>magnifying glass</u>, some <u>white paper</u>, and <u>little
jars</u> for collecting the sand.

1. First collect some sand very near
the water. Then collect some very far
from the water. Look at the grains with
the magnifying glass. You will see that
the smallest grains came from near the
water. This is because they are lighter.
The waves carry them back toward the
water.

2. Now look for places where the sand is
black. This is usually near the sand dunes.
(Don't confuse black sand with tar on the
beach.) The black grains of sand are heavier
than light colored grains. So you find them
very far from the water.

3. Collect some of the black sand. Do it
carefully. Pick it up with your spoon and
pour it in the pan. You will probably pick
up some light colored sand also. Now cover
the sand with water. Shake the pan slowly.
The heavy black sand will sink to the bottom.
Keep taking the white sand off the top.
When you have mostly black sand left, pour
off the water.

4. Spread some of the black grains on a piece of paper. Now
examine them through your magnifying glass. Surprise! Some of
the grains will be different colors. This is because they are
made of different minerals.

194

CREATE A PICTURE WITH SEAWEED

There are many different kinds of seaweed. Some are very beautiful. Of course, they don't look very beautiful when they are all bunched up on the beach. But look at them through your "snooperscope." You can see them waving about under the water. They look very different.

You can have a lot of fun collecting seaweed and making pictures with it. Just follow our instructions.

Equipment You Will Need

A can or bucket   A piece of plastic   A newspaper
A piece of cardboard A large tray or pan

What to Do

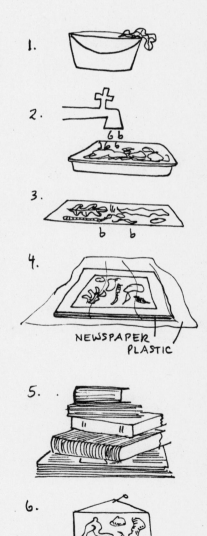

1. With your bucket, scoop up a few pieces of seaweed from the water. Only pick the pieces you think are pretty.

2. Bring the seaweed home. Rinse it with fresh water in a large tray or pan. Don't rip the seaweed.

3. Put a piece of cardboard under the seaweed. Lift the cardboard up. Do this carefully so that the seaweed is spread out all over the cardboard. Let the water drain off for a few minutes.

4. Lay the cardboard and seaweed down on a newspaper. Put some plastic over the seaweed.

5. Then put more newspaper over that, just like a sandwich. Put lots of books or other heavy flat things on top. This will flatten the seaweed. Leave it there for a while to dry. The seaweed will dry faster if you change the newspapers a few times.

6. When the seaweed is dry, it will be stuck to the cardboard. Hang it on a wall like a picture.

LEARN ABOUT SOLID WASTE AT THE BEACH

What is <u>solid waste</u>? It is something that is <u>solid</u> and <u>wasted</u>. People throw out a lot of solid waste. You probably call it garbage.

Nature isn't like people. Nature recycles its garbage. Dead plants and animals decay. They become part of the soil again. Or they become food for other living things. Nature doesn't <u>waste</u> things.

Turn over a dead fish or a piece of rotting wood at the beach. Examine it. You will see many little insects scurrying about. Watch seagulls picking at dead fish and shellfish. This is a natural process.

But nature has a hard time recycling the garbage people create. People's garbage litters our beaches. It pollutes the air and water at the beach. It harms plant and animal life.

Next time you are at the beach, try some of the activities we suggest. And think about ways that you can solve some of the solid waste problems at the beach.

Recycle your soda cans. Put litter in litter baskets. Nature isn't wasteful. People shouldn't be wasteful either.

Go on a Solid Waste Scavenger Hunt

1. Walk up and down the beach. Collect ten examples of solid waste. Pick some examples of nature's waste and some examples of people's waste.

2. Which of the things you collected are made by people?

3. Which are <u>natural</u> objects?

4. Which things did you see the most--objects made by people or natural objects?

5. Look at each object. See if you can figure out how it got on the beach.

6. Look at the things you collected again. What do you think will happen to them if they are left on the beach for a long time? Will any of these things become homes or food for animals? Will any become part of the sand? Will any look the same after a few months?

Which things are broken?

Which things are worn down?

Which are starting to rot or rust?

Which have tiny holes?

Are there any that aren't changed at all?

Metals on the Beach

Some beach litter is made of metal.
These metal things are ugly to look at.
Their sharp edges can harm people and wild-
life. But some metals are worse than others.
Try these activities. You will need a mag-
net. Use gloves to pick up sharp objects.

1. List some of the metal things you see on the beach.

2. Which of these are rusting?

3. Which have not started to rust?

4. Can you find a can that has rusted in one place and not
    rusted in another?

5. See which metals are attracted to your magnet.

6. Which metals are not attracted to your magnet?

Metals that rust contain iron. Iron is attracted to a magnet. Iron comes from the earth. Iron will keep rusting until
it is part of the earth again.

Some cans are made of aluminum. Aluminum
will not rust. A magnet will not stick to it.
These cans will never break down and become part
of the earth again.

Both kinds of metal litter are bad. It
takes a long time for cans made of iron to rust.
But aluminum cans will litter our beaches forever
unless they are picked up.

Did you find a can that had rusted in one place
and not in another? What was the non-rusting part
made of? Did it attract a magnet?

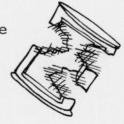

198

Sand and Solid Waste

Take Another Look at Sand

You will need:

A magnet   A small magnifying   A small dish or
                       glass   pie pan

Clean white
paper   Tweezers

Take some sand from the water's edge. Place it in the pie pan.

1. Look at the sand without using the magnifying glass. What do you see? List anything you can name or describe.

2. Look at the sand through the magnifying glass. List the things you can name or describe.

3. Wrap the magnet in a piece of paper. Then place it in the pie pan. The white paper will help you see more clearly what is picked up by the magnet. What do you think these pieces of sand are made of? (Remember what you just learned about metals.)

4. If your magnet is powerful, try this activity. Tie a string around your magnet. Drag it around in the sand. See how many little pieces of iron you can pick up.

5. Can you find any things on the beach which might become sand someday?

6. Could you say that sand is partly made up of solid waste? Why? What kind of soda cans will become part of the sand some day? What kind will never become part of the sand?

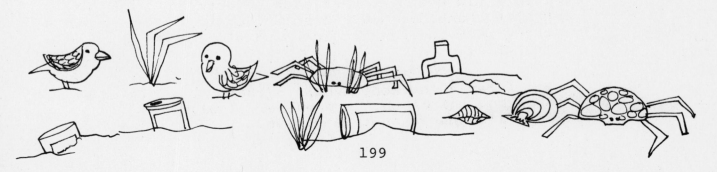

Make Your Own Landfill

Do you remember what a landfill is? It is a place where solid waste is buried in layers and covered up. You can use some of the things you collected on your solid waste scavenger hunt at the beach to make a mini-landfill. Studying the landfill will help you learn more about people wastes and natural wastes. Read more about landfills in the chapter "Where Does All the Garbage Go?"

1. Bring a large glass or plastic jar to the beach. It should have a wide opening so that you can put things you collect into the jar. (If you don't have a large jar, use a strong, clear plastic bag.)

2. Put some wet sand at the bottom of your container.

3. Collect things on the beach that were made by people. Put them in the bag or jar. Keep adding sand so that things you collect are buried in the sand. List the things you collected. Make a note about how they looked.

4. Now collect things from the beach that <u>come from nature</u>. Bury them in the sand also. List the things you collected. Make a note about how they looked.

5. Make sure the sand in the container is moist. Add more water if necessary. Then close the container tightly.

6. Bring the container home. Store it somewhere so it won't be disturbed. Open it every week and sprinkle some water on the sand. The top of the sand should always be moist.

7. Every few weeks, empty the container into a big box. Look at each object. Has it changed? How? Then put everything back in the container and close it again.

8. After a few months make a chart to show how things that are buried in your landfill change as time passes.

CHAPTER TWENTY SIX

Winter Changes

Like all seasons, winter is a time of change. In spring and summer living things grow. When fall comes the growing stops. In most parts of our country, the weather turns cold and the earth settles down for a long nap. This season of rest is important in nature's plan.

WINTER   SPRING

SUMMER   FALL

To many of us winter means snow, hail, and sleet. It means building snowmen, having snowball fights, and speeding down hills on sleds. In some parts of our country winter is not so cold. But it still brings cooler weather.

Winter comes because of the way the sun shines on our part of the earth. In summer, the sun's rays are hitting us directly, from high in the sky. But in winter the sun is low. Its rays are not as direct and hot. So we have colder weather.

By the time winter comes, living things have gone through many changes that will help them survive until nature brings spring again. This chapter will help you recognize the winter changes all around you.

TREES IN WINTER

One of the biggest changes we see when winter comes is in the trees. As cold weather approaches, the leaves seal themselves off. They stop making food for the tree. Soon they die and drop off.

During the growing season, food has been stored in each tree's trunk. Now water from the roots, which used to go to the leaves, is stored also. Soon the ground freezes and the tree must survive on its stored supplies. The stored food and water help the tree go through winter rest, called dormancy. When spring comes, young leaves will appear and the tree will awaken to a new season of growth.

PLANTS IN WINTER

Small plants change in cold weather, too. Perennial plants, like trees, live through the winter. They store food and water in thick, underground roots or in woody stems. Perennials will grow again in spring.

But not all plants are able to live through the winter. Annual plants die, and only the seeds they have produced live to become new plants in the spring.

To see what a seed looks like inside, look at a lima bean. Remove the outer coating. Break the lima bean in half. Do you see something that looks like a tiny plant? The new plant will grow from the baby. The baby is called an embryo.

BIRDS IN WINTER

Birds have a hard time in winter. They do many things to prepare for the change in seasons. Before the cold weather comes, they slowly begin to lose their feathers. This is called molting. The new feathers that grow back are softer and there are more of them.

When the birds separate the feathers with their beaks, layers of air get between them. These layers provide insulation from the cold.

Birds have trouble finding enough to eat in winter. They can't find many insects. The fruits and berries on plants are soon gone.

Many birds cannot survive these harsh conditions. They fly to warmer climates to spend the winter. You may see huge flocks of birds every fall, flying to the south. In the spring, you see them flying north again. This is called migration.

Not all birds migrate, though. Some stay right where they are. They eat the eggs that insects lay. They also eat the seeds of plants.

You can help birds live in the winter by making a bird feeder. An empty bleach bottle makes a fine one. Cut the sides out and hang it from a tree with a cord. Put bird seed and peanut butter in the feeder. Be patient--sometimes it takes a while for the birds to discover your treat. But soon you will see many different birds enjoying the food.

You can make many kinds of bird feeders. Read the chapter "Birds in the City" for a good idea.

INSECTS IN WINTER

Most insects die at the end of summer. The eggs that they lay contain the new life that will be born in the spring. Insects lay their eggs under the bark of trees or logs. Sometimes these eggs hatch into <u>larvae</u> and live through winter in that form. The eggs and larvae provide some of the food for birds who do not migrate.

But some insects do live through the winter. They hide in the ground and under the bark of trees. They become as cold as the snow. They remain quiet until warm weather comes again. This way, they do not need food. On sunny winter days, these insects may become warm enough to come out of hiding. Have you seen flies near sunny windows in the middle of winter?

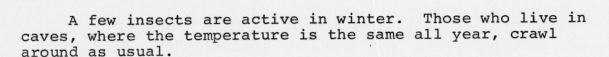

A few insects are active in winter. Those who live in caves, where the temperature is the same all year, crawl around as usual.

Insects such as fleas, who live in the fur of animals, live their normal lives. Bees move around in their hives all winter to keep from freezing.

Some insects even migrate! Orange and black Monarch butterflies travel thousands of miles to the south to spend the winter in warm climates with the birds.

204

ANIMALS IN WINTER

Most animals stay where they are for the winter. They don't migrate. But they must make many changes in the way they live in order to exist through the cold. Some animals sleep until spring in deep underground burrows. All parts of their bodies slow down. You would almost think they were dead. Woodchucks, frogs, toads, and snakes all survive this way. It is called hibernation. Hibernation is a long, uninterrupted sleep, without eating.

Other animals, such as chipmunks and bears, also go into a deep sleep. But since they wake up sometimes to eat, it is not true hibernation.

The animals that do not sleep have a difficult winter life. Most of them grow thick coats of hair to keep themselves warmer. Deer grow special winter hair. It is hollow. Air gets inside the hair and helps insulate the deer against the cold.

Food is scarce in winter. Squirrels dig up the nuts they buried underground in the fall. Foxes hunt for miles around to find a few squirrels and rabbits for dinner. Deer survive by nibbling dead leaves, twigs, and whatever dead grass can be found. By springtime, animals are lean and hungry. They are glad when growth begins again.

PEOPLE IN WINTER

We have seen that the living things around us go through many kinds of winter changes. We have learned about changes in eating, changes in outer covering, and changes in activity.

But what about <u>you</u>? Do you do things differently in winter? Are <u>people</u> part of winter changes?

People who live where winter is cold keep warm by putting on heavier clothing. We wear hats, sweaters, coats, and gloves when we go outside. Clothes help to keep heat from leaving our bodies, so we can be comfortable. Instead of wearing one piece of clothing, people wear many layers, one on top of another. These layers trap air to <u>insulate</u> our bodies. In this way, we are just like the birds.

People also eat warmer food in the wintertime. Think of the difference between the cold food you eat in the summer and the soups and other hot dishes that are so good in the winter. Hot food helps the body do its job of keeping you warm.

People spend a lot of time indoors in winter. We want to make sure that cold air doesn't come into the house. Houses are insulated by special materials under the roof and between the walls. Extra windows, called <u>storm windows</u>, can be added. Windows and doors can be sealed with a piece of felt or metal called <u>weatherstripping</u>.

The changes people make to keep themselves warm in winter take time and effort. Some people don't want to go to all the trouble of changing for winter. They make a different kind of change. Just like some birds, they go south for the winter! But most of us stay right where we are.

Index

Some Information
About the Environmental Action Coalition

On April 22, 1970, America celebrated its first Earth Day.
People paused to consider their environment. To enjoy its beauty.
To reflect on its problems. To consider the roles of government,
business, and individual citizens in preserving the beauty and
correcting the problems. Earth Day was a remarkable occasion.
In New York City the Environmental Action Coalition (EAC) formed
as a committee to coordinate the City's 1970 Earth Day activities.
Earth Day was the start of something big.

Following Earth Day the Environmental Action Coalition
became a permanent fixture. The non-profit, tax-exempt organization had realized that working toward a better environment is a
full-time occupation. From the beginning EAC focused its attention
on the special problems of the urban environment--particularly
solid waste. A network of volunteer community recycling centers
was formed to educate the public about recycling and resource
recovery, and to actively involve people in the daily process of
environmental improvement. Many of these centers are in operation
today.

But while working toward specific solutions to identifiable
environmental problems, EAC has realized, too, that in the long
term, it is an understanding of the environment by our nation's
young people that will ensure an environmentally sound future. In
this belief EAC has developed programs in environmental education
for children which include curriculum materials, visual aids, an
outstanding environmental library, speaking services, teacher
workshops, and Eco-News, a cheerful, informative, cartoon-illustrated
monthly newsletter about the environment for today's city kids.

If you are interested in obtaining further information
about the Environmental Action Coalition's educational programs or
publications, you may contact them at 156 Fifth Avenue, New York,
New York 10010.

218